Mariana M. Cooper is an intuitive life strategist, visionary, mentor and the internationally acclaimed host and Executive Producer of the *Aha! Moments Radio Show*, which has over 100 episodes on iTunes, and the *Aha! World Telesummits*, which reach over 85 countries around the globe. Mariana is also the founder of Aha! Moments International, a community and lifestyle brand dedicated to inspiring and educating people in combining the full use of their intuitive energies with practical strategies to live a truly enlightened life.

Mariana has an MBA in Marketing and a BA in psychology and spent over 10 years in corporate America as an executive and consultant working with businesses of all shapes and sizes in the Fortune 100, entertainment and non-profit industries, as well as with a myriad of small businesses and start-ups. She specializes in helping entrepreneurs, marketing teams and executives recognize their intuitive abilities and apply them in practical ways for creative problem solving and dynamic consumer marketing.

In addition to her formal business training and education, Mariana went on a quest to become fluent in the language of her intuition and apply it to everyday life. She studied with Dr. Doreen Virtue and was certified as an Angel Therapy Practitioner as well as an Advanced Medium over 12 years ago. She is a certified Kabbalist and a former Teacher with the Modern Mystery School, as well as a Jikiden Reiki Master. She is also qualified in the Silva Mind Method.

Mariana has appeared on radio and TV, and has published many audio and video courses. She is the author of *The Intuitive Living Oracle Cards*.

Join Mariana online at **www.TheAhaWay.com**

D0166848

THE *Aha!* FACTOR

HOW TO USE YOUR INTUITION TO GET WHAT YOU DESIRE AND DESERVE

MARIANA M. COOPER

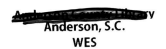

WATKINS
Sharing Wisdom Since
1893

This edition first published in the UK and USA in 2016 by
Watkins, an imprint of Watkins Media Limited
19 Cecil Court, London WC2N 4EZ

enquiries@watkinspublishing.co.uk

10 9 8 7 6 5 4 3 2 1

Designed and typeset by JCS Publishing Services Limited
Printed and bound in Europe

A CIP record for this book is available from the British Library

UK ISBN: 978-1-78028-936-6
US ISBN: 978-1-78028-892-5

www.watkinspublishing.com

CONTENTS

GRATITUDE

I am not sure where to begin. One of my mottos is, "It takes a village to get a book out to the world!" And that has proven to be very true.

This book has really taken on a life of its own and has had so many champions along its journey.

First, thank you to my agent Jill Kramer for signing me and being willing to work with a "new kid on the block." Also, I am so grateful to Watkins Publishing, including Jo Lal, John Tintera, the design, marketing, promotion and editorial teams and everyone who gave me the red-carpet treatment. Thank you especially for being so collaborative and keeping me involved in the creative process. That made this a wonderful experience. And thank you to the team at Penguin Random House for believing in this book and setting the stage for a great run.

Thank you to my producer, Sam Becker. You have been there for me on every show and you are truly my rock. Thank you for always making me laugh and keeping things going even when everything was blowing up around us!

Thanks to the "Real Writers," including Laura Bear, Julie Foster Hedlund and Gregory L. Norris, who put up with me in a very snowy Vermont retreat and took hours to convince me that I could do this too! Your ongoing support, advice, wisdom and love have been invaluable.

I am so grateful to my dear friend and extraordinary photographer Nikki Incandela, for an amazing shoot and getting just the right image for the US cover. I look forward to many more shoots to come.

Thanks to the staff of Barnes & Noble in Clark, New Jersey, who became my family as I wrote this book there day in and day out. You guys were the best support. Thanks for the chai teas, and your encouragement and willingness to help me procrastinate when I really was stir crazy and needed a good laugh.

Thanks to my friends and family, Mom and Dad, who put up with all of the ups and downs, mood swings, shutdowns and triumphs that come along with the creative process. I am so grateful for your love and support.

Special thanks to all of my teachers along this journey, especially Sandra Anne Taylor, Lee Carroll, Dr. Doreen Virtue, Carol Look, Allison Hayes, the late Dr. Alicia Stanton, Kere T. Atlan and so many more for guiding me along my way and believing in me.

I also would especially like to thank Dr. Dain Heer. Your unconditional care and attention have been the wind beneath my wings and I have jumped huge hurdles with your tireless support. For that I am so grateful.

And, finally, I say thank you to every client and audience member I have had. Without you all I would not have written this book. Thanks for your love, enthusiasm and willingness to always reach for something more. I hope that this book will be a help to you for years to come.

INTRODUCTION

Have you ever worked really hard to achieve something you truly desired and believed in, only to be met with self-doubt, constant obstacles, setbacks and confusion? Or felt like there was this quiet inner voice calling you forward but your logic and practical mindset swiped at it and killed the inspiration just as it was about to bubble over into action?

Perhaps you have flirted with the romantic notion of trusting your intuition and going for what you most want and even took action in that direction, but hit up against major detours or flat-out failure? Gun-shy became your middle name and mediocrity once again climbed into the wagon by your side.

What if I told you that there is a hidden language of communication that has always existed, holds all of the answers that you seek, always works once you know how to use it and gives you access to all of the inspiration and information you could ever want? And what if that language goes beyond what we traditionally refer to as intuition and is a comprehensive Energetic Communication System

(ECS) that you were actually born with which is meant to go hand in hand with your five physical senses of sight, hearing, taste, touch and smell?

What if that language could connect you to not only the subconscious part of yourself that is all-knowing and holds the answers to all of your questions, but also enables you to silently communicate with other people, your body, animals, the Earth and even other worlds? I know all this might sound far-fetched, but hear me out.

What if you have already been using this language without even knowing it, so with very little effort and just some simple directions, you could consciously begin to engage with it and provide rocket fuel for your ideas, longings, dreams and desires to bring them to fruition in record time?

Does such a language really exist? It absolutely does and not only were you born with it (there are no exceptions), but you have been using it all your life. It is what I refer to as your Aha! Factor. And I would like to assist you in turning yours on, tuning in your dial and tapping into the vast wisdom that is right within you, waiting for your attention.

Most of us were taught to pray or to ask for help in some way or another. And these systems of "asking" can be quite elaborate depending on which religion or modality you use. There are thousands of books and religious texts on how to ask, gain favor, cast spells, set goals and motivate us to "make it happen" or to behave in ways that will get us what we want. But there are not very many books on the language of "answered prayer." How do we get the answers? Wouldn't it make sense that if there are so many ways to ask and so many systems to tell us how to let our desires be known, that there is an equally robust communication system of how to interpret the answers?

Why would we not have some built-in way of receiving communication back from the energetic systems we are making requests to? The God of your understanding – your Creator, Spirit, the Universe, Source Energy or whatever entity it is that you are making requests to – has a very distinct way of communicating back to you. And this entity uses just about everything in your environment to do so. But just as if you are in a foreign country and do not know the language, you are missing the whole conversation. This does not mean that you are not getting answers. You just have not been able to interpret what they are, until now.

In this book I will be taking you from the often unpredictable and haphazard experience of a random glimpse of knowing, which we often refer to as our "gut feeling," to being able to fully ignite your Aha! Factor and apply it to the creation of your most meaningful desires. I will not only break down the anatomy of the popular "Aha! Moment" but I will share with you the missing pieces that make up the full spectrum of our Energetic Communication Systems (ECS). When we are fully aware of our Aha! Factor and how to use it everything in life gets easier and anything is possible.

I will also provide you with the pillars to what is referred to as Enlightened Living – a lifestyle that fully integrates our intuitive and energetic capacities with our mental abilities and physical actions, so that we are creating our lives with much greater ease and reliable tools that we can totally trust.

This book is going to help you to not only see, hear, feel and know that your hunches, musings and ideas are real, but it will also provide you with the super-easy formula of how it all works and what to do with it when it does. That other "voice" that you hear – the one that is a bit quiet but persistent and always seems to bring you back to the same place – is not simply there to guide you out of harm's way, but it is also meant to be a messenger between you and the world of all-knowing, of greater consciousness and of infinite possibilities.

Can you imagine how much easier complex projects, parenting, decision-making, being creative, relationships, understanding what your body requires, even choosing a political candidate would be if you could get the other side of the information (the energetic part) to go along with what you physically see and hear? How powerful would it be to be able to engage step by step with both the energy and the action as you sorted out a complex situation with a love interest or a new project at work? This is the natural, innate system that we all have but were never taught to use. It is what so many refer to, but not many explain.

When you finish this book your dreams and desires will be so much more accessible and you will have a reliable system to bring them to fruition – because you will be able to ask your Infinite Self questions and get answers that are backed up with the proof that they are real. It will be so much easier to make decisions and to take action, knowing that you have a built-in co-pilot leading the way!

A Powerful Realization

When I was in my late twenties my fiancé died. He was my best friend and a huge source of inspiration. He was in his twenties too and the whole thing just seemed terribly unfair. He had proven talent as a writer, director, dancer, choreographer, poet and a whole lot more. He had so much promise and it all vanished. I remember standing at his funeral and looking around at the cemetery. How rich was this soil? It made me look at all the people who had gone to the grave with their dreams intact. There were so many stories that had gone untold, so many songs that had never been sung, dances that had never been danced and inventions that had never been made.

It is not my intention to dwell on the negative, but what I realized then, at such a young age, was that we all have something major to contribute in life and so many of us never do. I don't think that laziness, apathy or some of the other unforgiving labels people put on it are necessarily the reason that we don't manage to reach our goals and manifest our desires. My feeling is that so many dreams never come to life because we are systematically told that they don't particularly matter. And that apathy stems from feeling frustrated that we can't access all of the information, tools and resources that we need to bring our creative ideas to fruition. We have been operating with less than 50 percent of what is available to us when we rely simply on logic and our mind, and we don't engage our Aha! Factor.

We are told that we should focus on the achievements that society, our parents, our friends, our family and the media deem worthy. And if those happen to match what we desire, then great! We are in good shape. But for the majority of people they do not match and so we push our true longings aside.

Early on in my career, after finishing graduate school with an MBA in Marketing, I landed a big position at a Fortune-10 telecommunications company, which was, by society's standards, a great accomplishment. Although I naïvely expected a corner office with big windows and lots of decision-making power, I quickly woke up to the fact that I was far away from the corner and the nearest window was down the hallway. Instead I had to share an office with another middle manager and was assigned projects that were not destined to make much of an impact at all. I knew within two days that I wanted out and that I was not a "corporate" type of person. I was outspoken, creative and driven. I really didn't get the "corporate culture" and definitely didn't know how to keep my mouth shut.

While others were plotting their path up the corporate ladder, I was plotting my path out. I started to ask myself lots of questions that usually come up for people heading into their retirement years. My questions were:

"Seriously? Is this it?"

"Who am I?"

"Where do I fit in?"

"What am I really passionate about?"

"How can I have my passions, make the money I need and have the time to do it all?"

"What can I do for a living that will really make a difference in the world?"

"How can I get out of here? And who would I disappoint if I left?"

That last one was really telling. Can you relate?

What Would Happen if I Followed My Inner Voice?

Essentially I was asking, "If I followed my own inner voice, the one that seemed to be screaming, 'Get out of here, there is so much more to life than this, you are wasting precious time here that could be used for so many other fun things,' who would I be letting down?"

My parents came to mind first. They were very hard-working and traditional in their values. And they were thrilled to see me get a "good corporate job with benefits" at the phone company. They had both sacrificed their lives for their family. And I was grateful for the privileges that they afforded me. But I could also see that once my sister and I left home, their empty nest was filled with a longing for dreams gone by that had never seen the light of day.

In all of my anxiety and that constant tug of "there's got to be more," I went to the place I always turn to for answers – the local bookstore. That was when the big bookstores with in-house cafés became popular. I would get my chai and read every book I could on sorting out the whole "follow-your-dreams-and-make-a-living-too" thing. I often found myself fist-pumping the air in joy as I read author after author who very defiantly stated that we all had a right to fulfill our deepest longings.

But then I would get back to work or a family gathering and feel like I would have to go back into the inspiration closet and tone it down, so I would not disappoint anyone. The only thing wrong with that was that I was such a rebel, and at times when family or relatives would marvel and coo at my title and world-renowned company, I would just blurt out, "Yeah well, I hate it! And I have bigger dreams than that." I was then the catalyst for a huge spin of backlash telling me that my dreams were cute or admirable but they didn't really matter, that what really mattered was making a living and holding down the job.

I was told that I was unrealistic, that I wanted too much, that I was never satisfied, that I should settle for less and that my aspirations of having my own business and creating it as I go, of having a beautiful home that is a sanctuary, of riding horses, of dancing, of doing interior design, of painting and of doing all of the other things that made me happy were "nice but not necessary and should be put on hold until retirement." This threw me into a constant state of "I'll show you!" and I went on a quest to do just that.

In my rebellion I went off the tried-and-true path of parental plans, societal norms and corporate ladders, and blazed a new trail. I would go to the park and just sit and listen, thinking that maybe if I just got some quiet time I would get an idea of what to do next. And I was right. Whenever I engaged with nature, I came home and had a new download of fresh ideas to move forward with.

My absolute inability to live miserably in order to realize someone else's idea of what I should be doing pushed me to expand my intuitive abilities to guide me, since I really had gone off the beaten path. And as I pushed ahead, I started to connect to a system of communication that became so reliable and strong that I was able to find confidence and identify a process that I have come to rely on every single day.

Can you relate to any of what I am sharing? I am pretty sure that you can if you have picked up this book. And my desire is to share with you some perspective and tools that I used to create the life I had dreamed of.

My desire for you is that you come to know and trust that you really *do* matter, that your dreams do count and that with this new energy anything is possible.

I also want to show you some of the best ways to do this and provide you with the unique combination of core tools that will help you to use all the engines you were provided with in this lifetime. We are all pretty well-versed in the physical steps needed to reach a goal – there are plenty of goal-setting and motivational books, teachers and coaches out there. But there is a whole other side of ourselves that is actually the accelerator and fuel for those goals to come to physical fruition. This is the energy of what we call "consciousness." It is the interconnected energy that links us to everything else out there and provides us with both the seeds of inspiration and the directions, tools, opportunities and resources to bring it all to physical reality.

10

Most of the time we are operating with just our logical minds, with little to no real awareness of these special energy systems and tools that are available to us.

Like diet and exercise, when we put our logical minds together with our energetic systems, miracles happen – and pretty rapidly. And what's even better is that when we are working with energy, if we change our mind or want to go in a different direction, the transition is much smoother and easier than going at it all in our heads.

In this book I am excited to share a variety of discoveries with you, including:

- The reason why letting your dreams and deepest longings come to the forefront is so important to your overall wellbeing, and your friends and family, too.
- Why *you* as an individual matter so much – how to understand that there is a much bigger picture that you fit into and that your dreams are not only important for you, but also for the world at large, and beyond.
- To share the composition of your Energetic Communication System and how it all works, so you can see where your desires are originating from and why they can feel so strong at times.
- How your Aha! Factor is your most important Dream Acceleration Tool for achieving your

desires, and how to master it easily, enabling you to know what steps to take, when to push forward, when to have patience and how to trust the information you are getting enough to take action.

- How to identify and let go of or manage the inevitable dream-killers, naysayers and critics who try to sabotage your progress along the way.
- How to engage in your own version of "energetic hygiene" to clear the way for you to fully engage your Aha! Factor and receive what you desire.
- How to identify and remove any sneaky, hidden obstacles that may get in your way – some may surprise you.
- How to recognize when you are getting a sign from your energetic self, as well as 50 types of signs, symbols and synchronicities that you can watch for to know that you are on the right track.
- How to create your own personal Aha! Factor Toolkit that you can come back to and rely on 24/7 when you feel you may be getting stuck or need a boost in the right direction.
- How to apply all of this practically to create balance in your everyday life with much greater ease and lots of joy.

I really want this to be a fun journey for you, filled to the brim with Aha! Moments that make your heart sing. It can be challenging, I know, but guess what? Ignoring those inner longings and desires is way more difficult!

How to Enjoy This Book

First of all, take it at your own pace. It is pretty amazing to see how many insights and inspirations will come your way as you sync up your physical and energetic worlds. You may also find that things begin to happen fairly quickly, especially if you keep an open mind and take action on a regular basis.

Perfection Is *Not* Required

If you are like me, you are not afraid of hard work. In fact, you may be quite the opposite – you are passionate and driven and want big things to happen in your life, right? But one of the downfalls to that type of personality is that we have a tendency to feel like we have to be perfect.

Here is the truth: You do not have to be perfect! In fact I have found that even when I adhere just 50 to 60 percent to these principles, amazing things happen. And at 70 percent flat-out miracles appear. Your attention and faith are all that is required to get you going. So please don't blow your circuits by trying to be perfect.

Life is about being able to go with the flow. Engaging your Aha! Factor will provide you with the missing pieces that most of us don't have any idea exist. And when you finish this book you will find out how much safer it feels to roll with things as they come with your Aha! Factor, than to try to tighten up, control everything with just your logical mind and brace yourself to meet an unrealistic standard of perfection.

I can't wait to get you going because, once you see the capacity you have with your Aha! Factor in full swing, you will be able to create so much more in your life and engage all of your capabilities to bring your dreams and desires, both great and small, to fruition. And your joy, success and inspiration will make a huge contribution to the world at large.

We will talk more about this throughout the book, but for now grab a journal and a cup of tea or your favorite beverage and let's get started.

Chapter One

THE MANY VERSIONS OF YOU

There is a lot more to us than meets the eye. Most of us feel like we are just physical bodies with a thinking mind, and perhaps a spirit, which we have been told exists within us. This is fine but it leaves us with a lot of missing pieces that create a gap in our ability to fully maximize what we have available.

Basic Principles – The Lay of the Land

Before we get into the nuts and bolts of intuition and how it works, I would like to establish some basic parameters for you to be aware of. It is helpful to understand the nature of the "non-physical" world so that your mind can get a handle on how your Aha! Factor operates. And once we can satisfy your thinking mind, it will be much easier to receive the rest of the information here.

One of the most common obstacles to recognizing your intuition and Energetic Communication System is doubt that they exist and not understanding how they work. Doubt will really hamper the flow of your Aha! Factor.

Energy and How It Works

Everyone and everything is made up of energy. Whether it is your body, your car, your food or your writing instrument, all of it is made up of energy. If you take any of these and break them down to the smallest parts, you will see that they all break down into moving particles. Certain things vibrate at a higher level of energy than others. But we are all energetically connected to each other and to all matter.

Through my many years of spiritual study and working with texts and teachings from many different cultures, modalities and doctrines, I have found a few things are common across most of them. Let's discuss the most important basic principles that create the foundation of our energetic world and the internal landscape of how our intuition works to power up the Aha! Factor.

Your Infinite Self: You Are Bigger than You Think

Our Infinite Self encompasses our entire being, both the energetic part and the portion of us that is physical in this lifetime. Ultimately, we are each a giant ball of energy with both physical and non-physical or energetic aspects. To give you an idea, envision yourself without your body, as a ball of energy the size of planet Earth. This is the version of you that is infinite. It is the all-knowing version of you that reaches through all of the galaxies and has no boundaries. Your Infinite Self has access to everything that is available to you across all dimensions, as well as the power to source and create things not yet tangible in your physical world. It has the capacity to provide you with even greater solutions and opportunities than your mental mind can conceive.

This Infinite Self can do a lot of things energetically, but there are some desires, experiences and opportunities for profound growth that can only take place when the energy is in physical form. At this point your Infinite Self decides to have a tangible physical experience, and takes on a body for an incarnated lifetime as a human being.

What is interesting is that not all of your Infinite Self steps into the body. In fact, the majority of your Infinite Self stays out of the physical body and assists the embodied part of you to navigate its world. The Infinite Self sends inspiration, protection and intuitive guidance to the physical body throughout its lifetime in the vessel.

The pendulum of communication that swings between the infinite version of you and the embodied version of you is the language of intuition. I like to call it the built-in communication system that God uses to answer our prayers. It is the language that keeps us safe, inspires us and lets us know the true intentions of others. You may prefer to refer to it as your "gut instinct." It is also the language that delivers our intentions to the greater energetic grid to actualize them into physical creation.

We will talk more in depth about the language of intuition and the other components of your Energetic Communication System that make up your Aha! Factor in the next section.

The Energetic Grid: The Circuitry of Life

In addition to being infinite beings, we are also all connected on what is often called the energetic grid. This has been shown to me in channeling sessions and dreams as a massive web of light, like a cosmic spider web. This web is the substance to which we send our intentions and also the circuitry that interconnects all things, bringing our thoughts back to us in the physical world. Managing our activities on this grid is often referred to as "manifesting," "magnetizing," "actualizing" or "attracting."

This circuitry is very powerful and has another interesting distinction, which is that we as individuals are made up of the same energetic substance as the grid itself. So we are both the potter and the clay.

And that is why our intentions are so powerful. The existence of this energetic grid has been proven by science and reconfirmed by many sources. I suggest reading the book *Countdown to Coherence* by Hazel Courtney, who discusses fascinating facts about the science of spirituality.

Plugging into the Consciousness of All Things

The knowledge and understanding of this energetic circuitry is called "consciousness." This is when we are physically aware of the energetic framework in which we live. It is the art and act of operating in our physical world with energetic awareness. When we integrate physicality with energetic understanding we achieve consciousness, and from this place miracles happen.

Everything in existence is also on this energetic grid, interconnected and made up of the same components. This includes animals, plants and all things animate and inanimate. For this reason, the more we raise our awareness, the greater our ability not only to navigate our world, but actually to shape and create it as we go.

All the World Whispers

Due to our interconnectedness on the energetic grid, everything has the capacity to communicate and respond to our intentions. There are many instances and accounts of plants and trees, animals and objects communicating and responding to human intention. What we focus on with emotion expands.

One other characteristic of this energetic grid is that it is neutral and responds to everything like a well-tuned electrocardiograph machine (EKG or ECG). This means that as individuals we have a great influence on our bodies, our environments – both internal and external – and everything in our waking worlds. In addition, our interaction with others also registers on the grid, which carries our thoughts to wherever we direct our attention. This is why when you think of someone, they may call you shortly thereafter.

This is also the way that we start to experience signs, symbols and synchronicity in our world based on what we are sending out onto the grid with our thoughts, feelings and emotions. Our thoughts seem to originate in our minds and we then send them out as desires onto the grid to the greater consciousness. They are configured for the highest and greatest good of all concerned, both ourselves and anyone else involved in the ultimate outcome and then returned back to us – step by step – often through a series of interactions. Most of the time our desires have been upgraded by our Infinite Selves, and as long as we are open to receiving the outcomes, we get them.

Our Desires Originate in Our Infinite Selves

When we have a desire, it actually originates within our Infinite Self and then is passed into our embodied self via our intuition and other types of energetic communication. We receive it as an inspiration or an Aha! Moment. Our desires originate from what I like to call the vat of "Infinite Potentialities."

What you seek is actually seeking you! That puts a very optimistic spin on things, right? This is especially true if you allow yourself to consider ideas and desires that come from a genuinely inspired place within yourself, rather than something outside of yourself, such as the desires of other people who would prefer for you to do things according to their point of view.

The Group Consciousness

The energetic grid has access to and interconnects with everything and everyone. Because this grid joins us all, we are also all plugged into our group consciousness. And there are certain currents of thought that are very prominent. We are all big psychic antennae and can pick up on the thoughts, feelings and emotions of anything and anyone. This is both a good thing and a challenge.

It is good because we can go into meditation and tap into wisdom from outside of our minds, as it exists in

21

the greater consciousness. Artists, inventors, writers, musicians, teachers, speakers, athletes, surgeons and others attribute this to "being in the flow," feeling like they are being guided by a greater consciousness or an energy bigger than their own minds.

On the other hand, if we are not managing our focus closely, we can often pick up on group consciousness that is not positive. We can take on other people's negative thoughts – feelings and emotions that do not belong to us. This can become tiresome as we try to solve issues that are not really ours. However, because we are aware of the possibility that something is not really originating within us, we can remedy this easily by choosing to refocus on what we truly believe in and desire.

Your Personal Bull's-eye of Energy

Although we are all connected, we do have our own personal energy field that is in alignment with our physical bodies in our current lifetime. I refer to this personalized field as your Bull's-eye of Energy. Take a moment to envision a bull's-eye with three rings. Now, put yourself in the center of those three rings (see illustration below).

Aura – 50 feet (15 metres)

Your First Ring of Energy – The Aura

The ring closest to you energetically is your aura. It is the energy that emanates from within your body and extends out about 50 feet (15 metres) from your physical body in all directions. This extension is referred to as your auric field. It is the field of energy that is most personalized to you and your inner self. It is like your own unique energetic DNA.

No two auras are the same. Your aura carries your current mood, subconscious thoughts, intentions (both good and otherwise), as well as your conscious thoughts and emotions. It tells the world how you are feeling, what your true motivations are, if you are physically ill and many other personal things.

Your aura shifts and changes with every thought and feeling. You can telescope it out with your thoughts or pull it in close to you to protect your energy. When people have their auric field fully extended, they are usually outgoing, extroverted and in a lively type of mood. You know that they are there. This can happen both when someone is happy and positive or angry and negative. If, however, people have their auric field pulled in very close to themselves, they will come across as quiet, shy, introverted, guarded or shutdown. You can also deliberately pull in your own aura to protect yourself from negative thoughts or circumstances.

We are constantly interacting with the auric fields of others. So anyone within a 50-foot (15-metre) radius of us is sharing energetic space with ours! This is true even if there is a wall between you. It is why you can be feeling terrific and then when someone who is depressed walks into the room, you can start feeling down all of a sudden without even knowing what the other person is thinking.

As you get more advanced in tapping into and interpreting your Energetic Communication System and igniting your Aha! Factor, you will be able to discern the auric energy in the room and know if it is you who is having a particular feeling or if the energy is coming from someone else. This is especially helpful in business and love relationships. Being aware of what is your own energy and what is someone else's helps a great deal when it comes to navigating relationships and business interactions with others.

Soul – 500 feet (150 metres)

Your Second Ring of Energy – The Soul

The second ring of the Bull's-eye of Energy is the soul. It extends out 500 feet (150 metres) from your physical body in all directions. The soul is still distinctive to your individual self; however, it is the part of you that is called "multidimensional." Your soul is much more complex than your aura. It reflects not only your blueprint for this particular lifetime, but also the blueprint for all of your lifetimes and lessons.

Your soul interacts with the auric field of this particular incarnation as well as all of the other incarnations that you will have. In fact, each lifetime that you take on is an attempt for your soul to educate and elevate its own consciousness and enlightenment. It is very similar to a person working on several different projects in order to develop into a well-rounded manager at work. They may try a variety of different roles to develop their skills and talents, as well as to enjoy several types of experiences.

Similar to a person looking back over the breadth of their career and remembering the lessons they have learned along the way, the soul is constantly seeking to grow and take stock of what those experiences have provided in its overall evolution.

Spirit – infinite!

Your Third Ring of Energy – The Spirit

The third ring of the Bulls-eye of Energy is the spirit, the part of you that extends indefinitely. Spirit is the entire Universe and it is the essence of all things. This ring is what interconnects everything, both physical and non-physical, to each other.

The spirit is the interactive energy that you plug into to participate on the energetic grid. It is the energy that we are all made up of and it allows your soul to expand into the full multidimensional consciousness that enables us to access or create anything that we focus on. The spirit is the part of ourselves that we send requests and intentions to, the energy that we ask questions of and that sends all of our awareness, solutions and answers back. This is the energy that we can configure into anything we desire with our thoughts and focus. As you learn to master your Aha! Factor, this is the ring that will open you up to the most amazing and powerful experiences.

When you are aware of the power of these rings, it is much easier to master your intuition and consistently increase the engagement of your Aha! Factor.

Remember: Your Bulls-eye of Energy consists of three rings:

The aura – 50 feet (15 metres) out

The soul – 500 feet (150 metres) out

The spirit – infinite

What you need to know most about your Bull's-eye of Energy:

- The rings of energy are magnetic and attract everything that you experience.
- They send out everything you think into the Universe.
- The Bulls-eye is neutral until you program it.
- You have the free will and total control to program it and to attract anything that you desire or need.
- Through your focused thought, you are always programming the Bulls-eye.

Your Aha! Field of Energy in Action

When our logical minds can't think of an answer, we may assume that a problem is unsolvable. But that is when the Bulls-eye of Energy is activated through your intuition. If you ask a question and follow the steps that I will outline shortly, you will activate your Bulls-eye and it will start working for you. Your Aha! Factor will become discernible and easy not only to recognize, but also to utilize with focused and deliberate intention.

How My Bull's-eye Has Worked for Me

A few years ago, when I was really worried about the status of my relationship with my boyfriend, I quietened myself down and asked my intuition to tell me what was happening and what I should do. I asked, "What is the greatest truth about this situation?" I immediately felt a cool sensation and a sense of calm. Once I had finished making my request, I let go of the thought and carried on with my day.

While I was driving the next morning, I suddenly started to hear in my head the lyrics of a song by Frank Sinatra, "The best is yet to come, baby, and it will be fine …" Then I knew that this was a sign from my intuition that things would be OK. But like anyone else, I had doubts and said to myself, "Well, that could be wishful thinking; let's see if another sign presents itself." This gave my Aha! Factor the permission to bring me the true answers.

I later met a friend at our favorite Italian restaurant that night for dinner. And to my delight, exactly the same song by Frank Sinatra was playing in the restaurant! I felt very comforted and relieved. No action was necessary. But what was even more exciting is that on my way home from dinner, I was caught by a red light. And just as I stopped, a truck went by with a big sign on it that read "Expect the Best!" That was three times I had been told that the best was on its way! One of my mentors always said,

"If you see it three times, then it's a true sign!" I was thrilled and happy because my Aha! Factor was hard at work to bring me the answers. And yes, the best did come to pass – not too long after that I heard from my boyfriend and things between us smoothed out beautifully.

So once you start to consciously program your Bulls-eye with positive intentions, questions and requests, you will be very surprised to see how quickly your Aha! Factor will respond!

Chapter Two

YOUR ENERGETIC
COMMUNICATION SYSTEM

One of the most consistent things that I hear from speakers on my radio shows and telesummits at the beginning of their interview is, "Things have changed. The energy is very different now." And I have to say that I agree wholeheartedly. In addition to hearing such comments from the New Thought leaders, healers and channels who come on my shows, I have also heard similar comments from other leaders, such as Pastor Joel Osteen, the Rev. Michael Beckwith, Oprah and scores of others.

What is everyone referring to? We all know that technology has advanced tremendously in recent years, changing the entire way that we live our day-to-day lives. And while we have made a great deal of progress and have gained forward momentum, the shift has changed the load on the Earth and our environments, as well as our stress levels, how we take care of ourselves, how we raise our children, how we shop, eat, move and work, and so on. Things are so much faster now on so many levels and if we look beyond technology at other aspects of our society, such as policies on fuel and education, and our political and financial systems, we find similar "progress" has been made.

With all of these advancements there is a whole other level of things going on. And that is energetically. Our physical world that makes up what we consider to be our "tangible experience" has an entire system of energy in place that creates everything we perceive in our day-to-day lives. Just as our bodies have physical and energetic properties, so does our environment. What's interesting is that the very energy that fuels us is also the same energy that we use to create our experiences. In fact, this energy can be used to create anything that we desire and influence anything going on in our life, without exception. And it works whether we are aware of it or not.

Now many scientists have studied this energy and perhaps the most exciting results have been in the work of the quantum physicists, who have challenged and disproved aspects of previously accepted Newtonian science. The biggest discovery that was made was that whatever we observe, we can alter with our thoughts.

But let's bring things back to a personal level. You have a huge system of support that was intended to assist you in the navigation of our complex physical world. For each of your physical senses there is an energetic counterpart that you were born with and that can provide you with protection, inspiration, new creative ideas and much more, including the capacity to consciously interact with your Infinite Self, your body, other people, animals, the Earth and beyond.

This system starts with what is commonly known as intuition, but the Energetic Communication System that I am referring to here goes way beyond the tenets of intuition. You have so many more capabilities than you know!

As we discussed earlier, we have all been created with a built-in operating manual that was meant to help us live at full power and not only navigate our world, but also use the very energy that we are comprised of to create the lives we desire. When you fully engage the different layers of the Energetic Communication System and learn how to interpret them, you dramatically increase your ability to direct the situations in your life, create what you desire and access the full spectrum of your Aha! Factor.

So let's look at what your ECS consists of:

1. Your intention
2. Your intuition
3. Your telepathic ability – to both send and receive non-verbal thoughts with other people
4. Your channeling ability – to both send and receive communication with energies that are not in a body

5. Your capacity to receive and perceive both
    physical and energetic information in
    combination with each other and to navigate
    your world with greater ease

Your Intention

This is a very popular term these days and one that
has become quite mainstream. Your intention is very
simple. When you set an intention you are making a
choice. We all choose each and every point of view we
hold, even when it seems like we do not. In this case,
though, when we set an intention we are choosing
what we desire to have. Ultimately, it is a message
that we send into the energetic grid of creation via our
recurring thoughts. Backed with strong emotion and
with focus and consistency, it manifests as physical
matter or a circumstance that we experience in our
daily life.

Your Intuition

To recap, we are all a combination of our Infinite Self
and the part of our Infinite Self that is now experiencing
a lifetime in our body, our Embodied Self. Your Infinite
Self has a language that sends messages, information

and guidance to your Embodied Self and that is called your intuition.

The language of intuition is made up of four energetic senses that overlay your physical senses. These are called "The Four Clairs": Clairvoyance – energetic sight; clairaudience – energetic hearing; clairsentience – energetic feeling; and claircognizance, energetic knowing. We will be looking in detail at how this all works in Part II, but for now, it is sufficient to recognize that it is always through these senses that your Infinite Self will first communicate with you. Your Infinite Self will also engage your physical body and environment to reinforce the energetic guidance that it is sending.

Telepathy

Now let's go a step further. One of the most popular things that we hear when it comes to energy and spirituality is that we are all connected energetically. And this is true. So wouldn't it make sense that there would actually be an energetic communication system that we are able to use non-verbally with each other? Of course – and there is! It's known as telepathy. Most of us have heard the word but usually regard it as a parlor trick that is used by stage magicians.

But telepathy is way more than a parlor trick. We all use it every day. Have you ever sensed what another person is going to say before they say it? Or felt that your pet was not feeling well and when you came home you discovered that they were in fact sick? Have you ever sensed that someone you care about was going to call or tell you something and when they did you said to yourself, "I knew that was going to happen?" Often mothers and their children communicate this way. These are just a few ways that let you know that your telepathy is engaged and doing its job.

Incidentally, telepathy is also the way in which animal communicators speak to animals. Members of the animal kingdom speak to us telepathically with pictures and once you know how to perceive that energy you can have a much deeper level of connection with your beloved pets and other creatures.

Channeling

The third part of your Aha! Factor is channeling. And that involves being able to have an energetic conversation in which we receive information from and interact with our environments, the Earth, our bodies and the plant and mineral kingdoms. Medical intuitives have a particular knack at being able to channel messages from people's bodies and we can also collect valuable information from our bodies by engaging our in-born channeling abilities. Channeling is also an ability to receive new ideas, inventions, hunches and information from other worlds for our own advancement.

Most inventors, tech developers, scientists, artists, writers and other talented people who create completely new ideas are channeling it from the energetic realm that interconnects not only all of us on Earth in this time–space reality, but also many other parallel realities. Sounds far-fetched? Maybe. But that does not mean it is not true!

When we engage our Energetic Communication System and activate our Aha! Factor at full steam, we have a complete set of tools with which to live so much more easily and efficiently than we do with just our physical and mental awareness alone. The Energetic Communication System is incredibly powerful and it offers you the ability not only to receive inspiration but also to bring that inspiration into tangible reality. Your ability to receive and perceive physical and energetic information in combination with each other will be one of your greatest assets when it comes to accomplishing all of the things that are important to you.

What Are We Supposed to Do with All of This?

With all of this equipment both physical and energetic, doesn't it make sense that you have a lot to contribute to the world? As I considered what I wanted to share with you, I knew that I desired to explain the mechanics of how your Aha! Factor and your Energetic Communication System work and to help you to tap into the other part of yourself that we have, in most cases, not even known exists (or if we have known, had no idea of how to work with it). But I also felt that there is a much bigger reason to tap into and embrace your Aha! Factor. Why? Because *you* matter and *your* dreams count and when you are able to access all of your abilities, your desires will manifest more easily and the world will benefit tremendously from what you have to offer.

In the next section we are going to see just how important your dreams and desires are to the lives and progression of others and I would like to invite you to apply what you learn here to bringing your biggest aspirations to fruition and sharing them with all of us. With these innate abilities, both physical and energetic, to call upon, doesn't it make sense that you have a lot to contribute to the world?

PART I

YOU MATTER MORE
THAN YOU KNOW

Chapter Three

A WAKE-UP CALL

Before we get deep into the mechanics of how your Energetic Communication System works and how to apply your Aha! Factor to your big dreams and desires, I would like to ask you an important question: What brought you here?

Why did you feel the pull to pick up this book and start reading it? Over the years I have found that most people do not come to my classes, shows or private sessions because everything is going great in their lives. They are not starting our conversations with, "Mari, I have it all! Life is glorious and I am content with everything that is going on." Instead, most are coming because they feel stuck. Or they feel that something is missing. The symptoms that bring them to me often include: a lack of (or fear of not having enough) money, a problematic job or love relationship, the need for a new home or car, worry over business issues, confusion about the path their life is taking, concern over family relationships and parenting challenges or a stubborn health issue. While these seem to be the main problems at the surface, the big issue that underlies all of these concerns is a need for clarity. People come to me to get clarity and to help them to sort things out. They want to know how to stop the madness of the seemingly out-of-control and random nature of their lives.

When they hit upon those hard-to-solve problems, they are often at a point at which things no longer make sense the way they used to. They find that the solutions they have used in the past no longer work and they are feeling tired, frightened or frustrated. Does any of this sound familiar?

This is what is referred to as your Awakening. When we are attempting to understand why our old ways are no longer working and how we can fix things, we start to ask a different and deeper set of questions. When you begin to ponder these questions, you are going beyond the basics of how to get more cash or when your boyfriend will send the next text. You are walking through a big gateway that may seem daunting, but is extremely powerful and life-changing.

The Awakening is when we start to become aware of ourselves and what we are doing from a different vantage point. We start to turn inward when we can't seem to find the answers from our outside world. And as we turn inward we discover our "Observer," the part of us that can step back and watch us in action and then switch back into participating in our regular physical world.

This is a time when the Observer within us begins to let us know that it is time to engage our lives from the inside out. It is a time to grow and expand and to become aware of the Energetic Communication System that allows us to perceive and receive the information we seek from our higher selves, as opposed to from the world at large. During our Awakening we start to feel very different from those around us and from society. It often feels that the way we have been living – no matter how "normal" and accepted by society – is not working for us anymore.

Invitations to awaken show up in the form of many different types of life events, such as:

- Failed relationships
- Unrequited love
- The death or loss of a loved one
- Job loss
- Divorce
- Health challenges
- Stubborn weight issues
- Substance abuse
- Hitting rock bottom
- Wanderlust

These are just a few examples and often during an awakening period we experience several of these in combination with each other simultaneously. When this happens we call it the "dark night of the soul."

This can be a very disconcerting time when it feels like everything is going wrong. And it can also be quite frightening if we don't have an awareness of the tools we have to help us.

When we go through this type of challenge, at some point we stop and realize that we can't do this alone, that we are at a loss of what to do. And after some panic and spin we sink into quietness. We start to ask the tell-tale awakening questions such as:

- What is going on?
- Why are things falling apart?
- Why is nothing working?
- Why am I so restless?
- Who am I?
- Where do I fit in?
- Why doesn't anyone "get" me?
- Am I the only one who feels this way?
- Why am I doing this?
- Why am I so different?
- What if the "normal stuff" just doesn't feel right anymore?
- When will I be happy?
- Am I selfish for wanting more?

These are just a few of the awakening questions that drive us to probe deeper and to turn on our Energetic Communication System in our conscious minds. Can you relate? I know that I still ask some of them myself because once we are on the path of consciousness, we are always evolving into even greater versions of ourselves.

The awakening questions and the anxiety that they bring up usually gives way to what I refer to as the Quest. We start to embark on a journey that we may not be sure of but feel strangely pulled toward. And we also have a burning necessity to make sense of our lives and get clarity on our direction. So we turn to books, Oprah, magazines, therapists, healers and the like. But how do we know what is right and what is wrong for us? How do we get the courage to blaze our own trail? How do we give ourselves permission to be a pioneer and create as we go? And who are we to go off of the normal path? Who are we to think that our ideas, our dreams, our inner longings really matter? Do *we* really matter?

One of the biggest reasons that we can get into an excruciating tailspin is that we have a really hard time perceiving the answers that are coming our way. That is where your Aha! Factor comes into play. Every time you ask a question, you are getting answers from your energetic grid through your Energetic Communication System. In fact, the way in which we turn on the engine of our ECS is to ask a question. Our Infinite Self cannot go against our free will and cannot provide us with solutions unless we ask. So the fact that our awakening incidents have driven us to ask so many questions is perfect for getting a flurry of insights and answers to come our way.

The Biggest Roadblock of All

Before we get into the mechanics of enlisting our Aha! Factor and firing up our Energetic Communication System, I want to address the biggest roadblock people face when it comes to achieving their dreams – feelings of unworthiness. It would be unfair not to address this issue very early on, because this one thing can shut down your ability to perceive and receive answers from your Energetic Communication System.

Unworthiness is disguised in many ways and it is the kryptonite to energetic receiving, to the physical attainment of what we desire and to overall success in all aspects of our lives.

You Really Do Matter

One of the most detrimental hidden obstacles to receiving true guidance from your Aha! Factor is perceived unworthiness. So many people feel that they wish to trust their intuition and gut feelings – they know what they want, they request it, but then they get stuck. Maybe they procrastinate or find that even though they get an answer, they don't act on it.

This was a big point of confusion for me. I remember speaking with one of my spiritual mentors about how blocked I had been feeling as I tried to find the inspiration to move forward in my career. I couldn't understand why I was so stuck after I had worked so hard for so long. I kept saying, "But I have done this and this and I have been certified in that and educated in the other, and I have so many experiences and accolades to show for it. But I am not moving to the next level."

He listened with compassion and simply replied, "Mari, there is a big difference between worthiness and capability." He then moved on to another topic. I was so awestruck by that comment. It was absolutely an Aha! Moment. Capability is what we achieve. We prove ourselves with our certificates, credentials, accomplishments, contacts and people who endorse us. I come from a well-educated family and have several degrees and certifications of my own. In our family, education was imperative and titles, achievements and noteworthy accomplishments were seen as "rites of passage." Our capabilities were used to dictate whether we were "worthy" of moving to the next level. But this was a misuse of the word "worthy."

What I realized upon further reflection was that all of those titles and achievements had nothing to do with my worthiness to receive. Rather, they related to my capacity to do the next level of a job or to move forward on my path in some way. They were what I was "capable" of, not what I was "worthy" of.

Worthiness, on the other hand, comes from a totally different place. Worthiness is non-physical and has no true association with accomplishments. We come from the perfection of the Infinite. Our Infinite Self is born fully worthy and that is a distinction that does not have to be earned or fought for. Instead, it is a Divine right that just needs to be recognized. It is the balance of giving and receiving. If capability is our capacity to give, worthiness is our capacity to receive. And therein lies the balance that brings us true success and overall contentment.

One of the most important keys to mastering your intuition and receiving what you most desire is recognizing that you are worthy of having what you want. Although most people feel that you have to

The Water Cycle

earn worthiness, the truth is that worthiness cannot be earned. It is your birthright. Everyone is born worthy! Let me illustrate this more clearly. Take a moment to visualize the ocean. Now, imagine the vapours of moisture from the ocean evaporating and becoming clouds. The clouds fill up and transform into rain and the rain then falls, becoming part of the ocean. Although four transformations have taken place, the core substance of all four processes is H_2O – water.

Now imagine that the clouds are spirit, and the rain is the physical vessel (the human being) that comes to Earth, which is the ocean. Once the time on Earth is complete, the person ascends back into the whole of spirit, just as the ocean evaporates to create the clouds. We are all of the same energy as spirit, changing forms as we go through the infinite process of life. If we are all spirit in energy and essence, we are all worthy regardless of what we do or accomplish.

So the point to remember is that you are born with an infinite amount of worthiness, simply by showing up! And no matter what you do or how capable you are, you cannot be any more or less worthy of deserving what you desire. Anything that you desire is what your Infinite Self has inspired you to desire, so why would it not be available to you? And if that's true then why does it take so long?

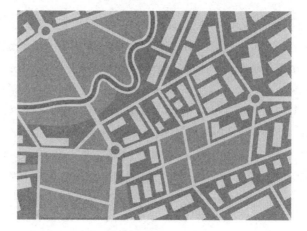

Your Aha! Factor Roadmap

We are all on a path whether we believe it or not. However, in the majority of cases, we have most of our paths mapped out for us in their entirety ahead of time. When we start school, we know that if we finish elementary school, we go on to high school. After that many of us go on to college. When we apply we are told about all the steps that we have to follow and the classes we have to take ahead of time in order to graduate. If we complete them our degree is assured.

When we decide to take a trip, we look at a map on our GPS. It provides us with every possible way to get to our destination. Every potential route is visible on the map. We can pick the shortest route, the scenic route or the route with the fewest tolls or least amount of traffic.

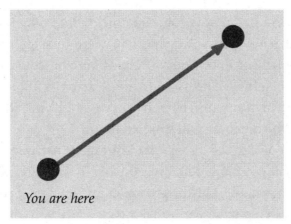

You are here

Our energetic map, however, does not work like this. Most people ask, "Well, if I have faith and believe, what do I get out of it? Show me and then I will invest the time in getting there." We try to apply our earthly ways to energetic principles. This does not work.

When it comes to your "Aha! Roadmap," the better example is that of a shopping mall map. The first dot says, "You Are Here." The rest of the map is blank, except for the one dot that represents your next step. That dot is not your ultimate destination, but the next step that your intuition is guiding you to take. You are required to step forward in faith to that next step. Once you do so, your next dot will appear.

If you step forward again rapidly in faith, the next dot is revealed even quicker and so on. As you learn to trust the guidance of your Infinite Self via the language of your intuition and become more consistent in stepping forward in the knowledge that it will not steer you wrong, the dots come so quickly that they form a direct path to exactly what you were in search of or to something enormously better than you could have ever imagined. This is your Aha! Factor in full action. It is always at work, even if you cannot physically see what the outcome will ultimately be.

As you can see, having the courage to ask questions gets things going. Being worthy of what we are asking for is our natural birthright and a given when it comes to deserving what we are asking for. Once you consider how efficient your ECS is and how the roadmap works, it all starts to make a bit more sense.

It can be good to be different – in the next chapter we are going to explore an unconventional yet very efficient way to attain your dreams.

Chapter Four

AN UNUSUAL APPROACH TO BRINGING YOUR DREAMS TO FRUITION

There are tons of approaches to making our dreams a reality. While writing this book, I was on a group call with a business coach and mentioned the title of the book. She curtly said "Oh, I'd change that. No one needs another book on fulfilling dreams." I was a bit bothered by her comment, more by the tone than the content. It seemed pretty ignorant. Have everyone's dreams come true? Is everyone on the planet confident and happy with what they are doing for a living? From my experience with thousands of clients, radio show and telesummit audiences, as well as social media, I can say an emphatic no.

Most people are wondering on a daily basis what their life purpose is, if it will ever come to fruition and whether or not their desires are truly worthy of attention. Everyone has a right to their own opinion, but this dismissive statement was shortsighted and I always trust my own intuition over someone else's off-the-cuff remark.

I have a very different approach to getting dreams to come true. And it is one which, when employed, will give you access to a huge vat of possibility that has been largely overlooked in more traditional systems. We are not going to focus on goal-setting, time management or even dream/vision boards and affirmations. When we just focus on the mechanics of goal-setting and the logical mind, we get attached to processes and outcomes, and lose access to the energy of the situation. Yes, I said "energy."

As we have been discussing, we are way more than just our physical selves and, as you continue reading, I want you to take the time to notice the energy as well as the physical process of what you are reading. Remember that the other part of us – the non-physical part – is infinite and accessible 24 hours a day, seven days a week. It has the capacity to make miracles happen. It communicates with us all the time through the language of our intuition, and it not only holds the key to the answers we seek, but it also puts the inspiration for what we want into our conscious minds in the first place.

To get you started on what could be a very complex explanation, let's break down what it takes to bring your desires to fruition into three basic parts.

1. **Inspiration:** This comes from our hearts, our intuition, our hunches, the greater consciousness, our Infinite Self.
2. **Communication:** This is the conversation between our intuitive senses, our logical mind and our physical world.
3. **Action:** This is when we take the steps we are guided toward in our physical world in order to manifest what we desire in life.

This process is a series of ebbs and flows. While we may focus on each part when we need to, it is not a good idea to fixate on just one element of the cycle. If we do focus only on one part, for example by meditating but taking no action or only using our logical mind without consulting our Energetic Communication System, we simply shut down our progress.

As we go forward I am going to share how we can combine our energetic capacities with our physical capacities so they have equal weight. For so long only a small percentage of people have been aware of the vast opportunities we can create when we are energetically aware and fluent in the use of our Energetic Communication System. These people seem to have great success – far beyond the average. Most of the time we say this is due to their intellect, who they know, how much money they have to work with, their family of origin, sheer good luck or some other tangible advantage. But in many cases such people have tapped into the success secrets of the ages and have learned that their intuitive fluency, energetic hygiene and mastery of working with the energy of pure potentiality lets them leapfrog ahead, way beyond any traditional means, and in record time, too.

These people can "follow the energy" and create as they go. They can allow for some things to remain open-ended – giving the Universe the space to make it even better, without a lot of physical effort. They seem to have a sixth sense about making decisions and don't fret if they have to change midstream, or if things suddenly turn in a new direction. They know that this is often the Universe stepping on the gas pedal and accelerating their dreams. They also know that sometimes, right before a dream is about to come to fruition – to come from energy, thoughts or visions into physical reality – things can often go chaotic or get very quiet, almost like nothing will happen. They recognize that this is just a time of transformation and this is when it is vitally important to power up the energy, not give up on themselves. This is what having faith truly is.

When you understand the various aspects that are really in play, how they operate and how they interrelate, you will see how much *power* you truly have and how much easier life can be. People have made a fortune by making things difficult to understand, complicated and confusing. But in this book I want to help you to see just how powerful you are, how to stop spending needless energy on the wrong things and how to put your focus in the right places to efficiently bring your dreams to fruition.

I am not saying that this is all a walk in the park, as learning to trust things that are new, different and often not perceivable to the naked eye can be a challenge. But once you understand the lay of the land and how it all works, you will see that you are able to plug into the true power source that creates all things and direct that energy in whichever direction you desire.

It is like having a toaster and a blender. If you tried to plug them into each other, neither would work. But if you plugged either into the wall, they would switch on and do their jobs, because they are connected to the electricity that powers all appliances. When we look outside of ourselves for our own power source, we are like that blender plugging into a system that cannot support it. Once you understand the power that you have at your disposal and where the true outlet is, you will be able to plug in and power up your entire life! It's like every appliance in your kitchen being plugged in and working to create dinner for a big occasion. And the best thing is, you have all of the tools you need built right into your body. So you don't have to acquire anything! I am just here to remind you of your energetic operating manual to go along with the mental and physical ones you kind of know already.

Chapter Five

WHAT YOU DESIRE, DESIRES YOU!

Now that we know all of the various aspects that come into play, it is so much easier to see that our dreams, desires and inner longings are not just coming from our own minds. When we feel inspired we are getting a summons from the greater consciousness, letting us know that someone out there is in need of what we have to offer.

As I wrote this book, I was often reminded by my guides that there were many people who were down and discouraged about their lives. They were feeling as if they should not speak up for themselves and that their inner longings were just one-way desires. The emotional pull of this group of souls would register on the energetic grid and I would get a passing idea that I should write a book about all I have learned on the topic. I got this message for years. And funnily enough, every time I sat down to write, I would hear this negative voice say, "Ah come on, they know all of this already," or "So many others have written about this – what you have to say doesn't really matter." The reality is that my negative rationale could not have been further from the truth! If it had indeed been such a ridiculous idea – one that no one needed or would have benefited from – it would not have kept coming up continuously.

You will know that the dreams and longings you have are coming from greater consciousness when you feel a very strong pull. How often do you get a hunch? How often do people mention their needs to you? How often do you see synchronistic events crop up that point right in the direction of your idea? When this happens, it's your Aha! Factor trying to get your attention!

While I was resisting writing this book, I was working with hundreds of clients and starting to see recurrent themes of where people were at with their feelings. Over and over I would hear, "I feel stuck, miserable, like nothing I do matters, like my dreams really don't count, like I just need to spend my time helping others get their dreams off the ground because I am not original enough or clever enough, or new enough or fancy enough or smart enough ..." – you get the picture.

In every session, on every radio show, at the end of every telesummit I would find myself encouraging people to step up, to follow their desires, because with this new energy anything was possible. I also found myself talking to them about becoming fluent in their intuition and how to communicate non-verbally with others or channel messages in their journals. My Energetic Communication System was teaming up with the group consciousness to let me know that there was a big need out there and that I was meant to fulfill it! And if you listen closely you will see that the same is happening for you.

You may be thinking that this is great when it comes to your life purpose or pursuing a passion that will directly influence or help someone else, but what about when you just want something such as a great new pair of boots or a flat-screen TV? That is a dream or a desire but how does that help others?

Well, it contributes more than you think. Here's the thing ... what you desire does not have to directly help others for it to be worthy of actualizing. We all deserve lavish abundance and opulence. There is plenty to go around and we do not have to ever think that because we acquire something, someone else will go without.

When you have a desire and you achieve it, the joy or relief or whatever upbeat emotion you feel sends out positive energy of hope, accomplishment and satisfaction to the energetic grid. This creates a lift for everyone – even if it does not register in their minds, it contributes to the energy of greater abundance for all. Similarly, if you say, "You know what? I prefer not to get that TV today. I am choosing to wait and save that money for something in the future or to pay a bill right now," that also contributes to the energetic grid and group consciousness in a positive way.

The point is that if what you choose lifts your mood – giving you a feeling of lightness, of joy or any other positive emotion – you are contributing something valuable to *everyone* energetically. What you desire, desires you too. And just knowing this should give you a boost of inspiration to take the plunge and move forward with your plans.

The other day I was in a great Italian restaurant in town with my friend. We looked over the menu and were really excited to see a variety of healthier versions of our traditional favorites, as this restaurant had more than 60 percent of their menu available as gluten free. While I was excited about the no-gluten option, my friend was counting the number of energy-boosting vegetables that would help her to stick to her dietary goals. We both chose delicious entrées that tasted exactly the same as our old, less-healthy favorites and were able to enjoy the meal fully with no guilt trips.

Now when we put this positive, self-empowering energy out onto the grid, we initiated a movement of self-love and self-care out there. Imagine if there was someone sitting across the room who was in a quandary about whether or not to break their diet, but all of a sudden, they got a little hunch to go with the healthier choice. Perhaps that extra bit of oomph came from us making strong choices and sending that energy out onto the grid that connects us all. This may seem "woo-woo" to some, however this is how it works. It's super simple.

Have you ever walked into a room and all of a sudden felt depressed or in a bad mood, when you had been feeling totally fine? Then you see someone who is having a very bad day or quarreling with someone else? We give out negative as well as positive energy, and many times it is much easier to discern the negative because we are more accustomed to it.

So, what if we could be conscious of what we are contributing to the grid? How powerful could you be in your own life knowing that your choices really *do* matter? What might you choose differently if you realize that every choice can be amplified for yourself and others? In the next chapter we will look at this in more detail.

Chapter Six

WHAT IF YOU COULD LEARN YOUR LESSONS THROUGH JOY?

Have you ever noticed most people believe that the hard and arduous path is the one to be valued most? That we are more virtuous, deserving or worthy if we are constantly struggling and slogging through our day or through life in general?

Being a bit of a rebel, I was never one to prescribe to the Puritan work ethic of work hard at all cost. It never made much sense to me. I mean, if I was miserable doing what I was doing, how could it ultimately be helping anyone? One of the reasons I was feeling this way was because I was always able to perceive another, extra energy, along with that of the physical action and the outcome. Being intuitive I could in almost all cases discern a person's true intention in spite of what they were saying or doing. And when I was in corporate America I felt so much heavy energy because so many people were denying their personal truths and toeing the company line, which in the short run might have made their bosses happy, but in the long run registered in the person's life as despondence, anger, illness, depression, passive–aggressive behavior or apathy. This in turn led to escapism through drinking, smoking, overeating, shopping and so on and formed a vicious cycle.

What was even more exhausting to me was how people were being financially rewarded for representing something they did not believe in. I am not saying this was the case with everyone across all jobs, but it was true of a notable portion.

This awareness led me to ask several different questions: "What if we could somehow learn our lessons through joy?" and "What if we focused on our natural gifts – which are our true strengths – and spent time fully embracing and developing them? Wouldn't that make more sense than trying to force people to keep doing what they were doing regardless of whether they felt fulfilled or not?"

I remember being in the career management division of Human Resources and teaching a full-day workshop on Managing Your Career. When I took over the job I promptly changed the title to "Taking Your Quantum Leap – There is Life After Corporate America!" It was consistently full, with a 100-person waiting list for a few years!

I was amazed at the exhausted state of the people who showed up in the room, with their glazed-over looks and well-rehearsed responses to my questions. I would ask, "What do you really want to be doing?" And in most cases they would recite the skills they were currently using in their job and how long they had been doing it. Then they would say that if they could just get a little more money they would be happy with that. I was appalled. I would respond and say, "Well, what do you dream about? What do you really aspire to?"

Again, I would get serious pushback. Everyone was so well trained to compartmentalize their true talents, dreams and inner longings away from their work. They believed that they did not matter and their dreams did not count. And in order to survive doing their job they would have to contort themselves mentally and emotionally to fit in and "make it work," biding their time until retirement.

I would then throw out the next set of questions: "What if you *do* matter? I mean, the real you? And what if your dreams, your desires, your values and your talents *do* count? What if you could learn your lessons in life through joy rather than hardship? What if virtue truly comes from how fundamentally happy you are and the energetic contribution that this makes to the world, instead of from the contortion of pent-up emotions around the sense of duty you think others want from you?"

This was regarded as a very strange way of thinking in the early 1990s – before the Internet, social media, blogs and all of the outlets to self-publish and pioneer the great ideas we have today. And while I got an initial backlash, I continued to ask the questions and offered them up for consideration. With persistent focus, and armed with a set of processes to help people see how this could come to be, things shifted. By the end of a class, people would be standing up cheering and feeling that they, too, had the tools to create balance and to move forward toward making their dreams a priority and putting together action plans to bring them to reality.

Now, before you get into a round of "yeah buts," "what ifs" and "if onlys" let me say this – it's a process! And what we are here to do together is to get you up on your feet and help you to move forward toward a new way of being. You do not have to quit your job or flip your life upside down. Your mind is very possibly spinning right now if you are feeling a ton of resistance to what I just shared. However that is fine. We are not trying to get you to do this alone. And you don't need to think up all the solutions yourself.

In fact, your mind cannot go through this transformational process by itself, the way many people believe. This is not about "to-do" lists, goal-setting and foolhardy risk-taking. If you are like most people, you have been operating mostly using your logical mind to carry out the action steps and have not been giving equal weight and consideration to the other side that accounts for more than 75 percent of your success.

That other side is your energetic and intuitive senses. The energy is collective – it takes everything and everyone into consideration collectively. Your intuition is personal and it is the language that specifically guides you in every aspect of your life.

These two things – your energy and your intuition – are not just condiments in your life, they are the *major* food groups. And going without them is like living on a steady diet of hotdogs and chicken fingers with no fruit or vegetables.

What I learned while I was navigating my corporate and consulting careers was that I was using both my intuition and the energetic grid as much or more than mental analysis and physical action. Once I understood this, I was able to propel forward with so much more ease and joy, because I was operating with a full engine, not just half of one. Life in general, and specifically dream attainment, is so much more efficient when you get access to all of your tools, not just a few of them.

By the end of this book you will see what we have at our disposal just by being born and understand how you can easily tap into what is available and integrate it with inspired action to create miraculous results in short periods of time, and with a lot less wear and tear on your mind, body and spirit.

The Aha! Factor Leads the Way to Finding Your Life Purpose

Let's talk about this thing people refer to as "life purpose." I have always had a fairly controversial opinion about what it is and whether or not we all have just one solitary purpose we came here to fulfill.

For a while all of the self-help books focused on the idea that we each have a purpose that we need to discover and when we do, we can work at and love it without any reservation, fear or doubt. The idea was that when we were acting according to our purpose, we would take the world by storm and never experience any competition or negativity. This concept was also mixed in with "following our passion," which meant turning something we loved into a business or a career so that, because we were so "passionate" about it, we would never have to really work a day in our life.

Just as with the low-fat and no-carb diet crazes and the sugar-free sweetener popularity phase, what started out as a basic set of sensible guidelines, turned over time into extreme fads. For example, a decade later we saw the long-term effects of the low-fat craze as many people experienced an increase in blood-sugar issues because manufacturers were replacing the fat in their foods with extra sugar to maintain a palatable taste.

The whole "life purpose" movement has taken a similar turn. I have been on this journey both personally and professionally for two decades and have worked with thousands of clients on following their passion, building businesses and changing careers. We have worked together from all directions, both pragmatically and energetically and some interesting patterns have emerged.

Most people are in search of what I call their "inner Oprah" – that thing or contribution that will make them a legend and recognized by the world as having made a big difference. I especially see this with writers, speakers, coaches, healers and other service-oriented individuals. There is a level that we feel we must reach in order to be considered "living our life purpose." After having the opportunity to see such a cross-section of people embracing their search for their life purpose I began to get some insight into the phenomenon.

First of all, I believe that we are all born with innate talents, gifts, contracts and agreements. No one comes into the world empty-handed. Everyone has distinct contributions to make. That being said, it is generally not just *one* solitary thing. Why? Because if you miss the boat on one thing there is something else you can contribute in an equally great way.

In most cases people get their first glimpses of their catalogue of talents pretty early in life. I personally found my passion for dancing at two years old and for riding horses at the age of six. But I also showed a tendency to be a leader and teacher, when I would lead the other children in dance class through the moves that they were not getting. And by the time I was 15 I was teaching riding to kids at summer camp. Those leadership instincts continued to grow and gave me the foundation from which to speak and teach on a worldwide level decades later.

But I also had very strong interests in marketing, business, interior design and a ton of other things. While my mother would often laugh at my multiple interests and tell me to focus, on a macro level I was collecting life experiences and learning about all sorts of things, because eventually I would have a role doing psychic and intuitive work, which required me to relate to people from all walks of life. The more I had been exposed to, the easier it was for my guides to speak in terms that my clients could understand, and from a variety of perspectives.

My wide variety of interests also helped me to relate to the confusion that so many people encounter when they try to discover their own passion, purpose and right livelihood. I have found that these are three distinct things, each having a unique meaning. However, they have been used interchangeably and this has created quite a bit of confusion.

Let's discuss each one in turn.

Passion: This is the raw energy that we feel when we participate in something that truly makes our heart sing. It is an emotion and it describes the fuel that overcomes obstacles and makes us feel joyful.

We are not going into the romantic aspect of passion here, but there is something related that is worth mentioning: with passion comes vulnerability. When we are passionate about something, we invest part of ourselves in it, and that vulnerability raises the stakes.

Conversely, when the stakes are raised, we know we are feeling passion because if something doesn't have high stakes for us, it is merely an interest. When we date someone and we feel a swirl of intense emotion, we want more and there is deep desire, but with that desire comes the strong possibility that we could ultimately lose them and experience deep pain.

So when the stakes are high, so is our passion. When the stakes are not high, and we don't feel vulnerable, we feel friendship instead and not the chemistry, the heat or the emotion that we experience when we are feeling passionate.

Purpose: Our purpose is an action that both contributes to us ourselves and also offers something to others in a meaningful way. We could get granular with this, but let's keep it simple and say that purpose is when we discover a category in which we can make a difference for someone or to something. We do not necessarily have to make money from what feels like it is our purpose. And we all can serve many, many purposes at various times in our lives.

Look at the role of a parent. The first major purpose of a parent is to keep their child safe and healthy.

Next we add in education and preparation for the real world. Then someday the purpose is to let their child be independent and fly. While we are busy parenting, we can simultaneously be volunteering for an animal shelter or other charity, we can be involved in helping out on the campaign of a local politician whose views we are passionate about or we can start a recycling program for our town. These also register as purposes that make a big contribution not just physically but energetically as well.

Right Livelihood: I think that "right livelihood" is a much more accurate phrase than life purpose. Right livelihood is when we find or create work that encompasses the chemistry of passion and the contribution of purpose, with the additional criteria that it generates income for us and is in alignment with what makes our heart sing.

Here is the key: right livelihood evolves as we do. What is best for you early in life is not necessarily great for you later in life. Sometimes you out-grow it. And that is OK! What is also important about right livelihood is the way the work is configured. It needs to be in alignment with your values, your natural body cycles and it must shape your day in an appealing way.

Personally, freedom is my number one priority. I feel very trapped when I have a regimented schedule; it shuts me down and makes me feel confined. So no matter how passionate and purposeful I may feel about a particular type of work or contribution, if it is out of sync with my freedom factor or too confining, it is not registering as right livelihood for me.

It is important to keep this in mind when you are exploring the dreams that you really desire to bring to fruition. Your dreams for right livelihood *must* include the consideration of the quality of life you require and desire in addition to the contribution, money, accolades and so on. That doesn't mean that you won't have to make some compromises, especially in the beginning. However, if you are aware of these principles you will be able to build your desires into the plan from the start and on an energetic level you will be able to qualify those desires. For example, instead of saying to yourself, "Oh please, God, find me something that I can do to make ends meet," or asking "What's my life purpose?" try asking, "Can you please show me the right livelihood that is really aligned with who I am, what I am passionate about and what feels true to my purpose to make a great contribution to others and the world at large?" You can even add, "Please also configure it to be aligned with my natural creative cycles and enable me to make more money than I know what to do with!"

When you program your Energetic Communication System with that request, you will see a flurry of things begin to configure. And your Aha! Factor will heighten your awareness that you are on the right track.

Ask Your Aha! Factor How You Can Contribute

Now that we have the whole purpose thing sorted out, let's move on to another big detail that is not normally shared when it comes to exploring why you matter so much. That is that we are all used as instruments to help each other. You are used as a blessing, an answer, a messenger, a teacher and sometimes even a warrior for others each and every day. This is a pretty big deal. Let's face it, sometimes life can get pretty hard. When we are going through a tough time or, even worse, a time when nothing seems to be happening at all, it can be easy to fall into the belief that we don't really make a difference.

We may be under the illusion that we are separate and don't matter very much in the grand scheme of things. This could not be further from the truth. Remember that your thoughts, emotions and feelings register on the energetic grid and are all contributing to the energetic current at all times – and it never turns off.

Beyond that, just smiling at a stranger or holding the door that extra second so it doesn't slam in a person's face is a contribution. You don't know how that person's day was going. You could have been put in that position at that specific time to show them kindness when they were otherwise being abused, or to be a beacon of hope on an off-day when all seems grim.

These are very subtle yet significant contributions. Why? Because they add up to something much greater. Think about it. You know how you feel when you get up in the morning and you're in a good mood: You make a great breakfast, get out of the house on time and even in rush hour traffic people are kind, letting you into their lane or picking up the keys you dropped because your hands were full? Then you get to work and people are congenial: Someone shows up just in time to fix the jam in the copier, your meetings are collaborative and things are generally in good shape. This is a day when you feel like you are in the flow. Your overall stress level is low, things are fine and all is well.

The flip side is when you get up late, start rushing, burn your finger on your curling iron, get into traffic only to realize that you forgot your phone and have to turn around to go back for it, and so on. You get the picture, right? And if you are already in a worried state of mind – say, grieving over the loss of someone dear or concerned about finances – the second kind of day I've described can feel a lot worse than it is. Likewise, if you are in a new love relationship, the first scenario can feel a lot better than it is in reality. We have all sorts of twists and turns in our days and an infinite number of variables that we take into consideration before we register it as a good or a bad day.

So the way people behave, respond and interact with you throughout the day makes a big contribution to how you feel, one way or another. And while it may seem silly, you really can make a difference in someone's day with the smallest of gestures. Think back to your childhood when you were in school. Can you remember one particular incident with a teacher that still stands out to this day?

I had a teacher in high school who used to grill us on our Spanish vocabulary. She was very tall, wore a lot of makeup and would poke her lips out like a goldfish, as she enunciated the words with emphasis. Her eyes were huge and she had big hair to go with them. She drove a blue sports car and would almost run people over leaving school. Looking back I can laugh, but at 14 I was terrified of her. I was a rather dramatic kid and she would scare me to death. My friend Denise would always laugh at me because when the teacher asked me something I would hold on to the desk and imitate her facial expressions as I responded. I didn't wear makeup like she did, but I definitely could do the goldfish lips better than anyone in the room.

After the traumatic quizzing, I always had a heavy feeling about having been publicly called out in class. It stuck with me. And I always made a point of being much kinder to my own students and not teaching in an intimidating way. In fact, my Spanish teacher taught me what *not* to do, so she served a great purpose.

This is something that often trips us up. We think that everything we go through that is not pleasant is negative. But that's simply not true. We are often being shown a better way, being taught about empathy, compassion or patience. So when I ask, "What if we choose to learn our lessons through joy?" I am not implying that you will never encounter tough times, but that there is a blessing to be found at all times. And when you can collect those blessings, the whole process of life becomes more joyful overall.

The bottom line is that good or bad, great or small, *you count*. And you don't have to do something monumental to prove it.

As we move forward now, I'd like you to take a closer look at your own life and consider what your passions, purposes and right livelihood are or could be. Then, as you learn how to engage the various parts of your Energetic Communication System, you will be able to apply it to this area and get energetic guidance on the best paths to focus on. Your Aha! Factor was specifically built to help you to recognize both what your personal talents are and what you can contribute to others as well.

Chapter Seven

ARE YOU WILLING TO SHARE YOUR DREAMS WITH THE WORLD?

Now that we have sorted out the difference between passion, purpose and right livelihood we can move on to the next exciting part of your journey: identifying your desires and preparing to share them with the world.

What are your dreams? Not just your career or job dreams, but your lifestyle dreams? How do you desire to live? What do you desire to experience? It is so important to give yourself and your dreams a consistent opportunity to be seen. Your Aha! Factor is here to guide you step by step.

It is funny how many people answer, "I don't know," when I ask this question. I believe that we always know. We have just been trained not to trust or express the answer fully to avoid being judged or told that it is not a realistic idea.

Two Keys

First, if you don't let yourself have a big vision you end up focusing on all of life's little pieces, with no direction. This creates stress, spin and feelings of despondence or numbness. We have a tendency to fill our lives with all sorts of little things that never add up to the bigger picture.

Have you ever tried to furnish a room without having a plan? You just acquire haphazard pieces and, while they may have function, the room ends up looking like a college dorm, even with good-quality furniture? That is because there is no core design plan in sight. No big picture.

Let's say it was a rainy day outside and you had a lot of time on your hands. I give you a 1,000-piece jigsaw puzzle to put together and let you know you have the entire day to do it. You would probably think that as long as you could have food, something to drink and a few breaks during the day that it would not be too hard to finish. But if I told you there is one catch, and that is that I am going to take away the picture on the box, you would probably protest that you need a lot more time to finish, with no vision of what the end result should look like, right?

Most of us handle our lives this way. We stop our big visions because they seem impossible and then we spin around with all sorts of pieces that never really add up. And the worst part of it is that the feelings of numbness and apathy that result go into the energetic grid and create a bit of a down current.

On the other hand when we allow ourselves to really embrace our ideas and create a big vision for ourselves, we infuse positive vibration, hope, joy and create powerful magnetic energy that begins to configure the people, resources, opportunities, big breaks, acceleration and all sorts of other good stuff that will work in our favor.

The second key is to allow your Aha! Factor and Energetic Communication System to be major players in guiding you along the way. We will learn the mechanics of how to do that later in the book, but for now you want to have your ideas ready so that when we start to engage your energetic senses, you know what you want to really focus on.

Once you have the vision and put it on paper, you will be able to delegate a chunk of it to your Energetic Communication System to let you know what is good, not good, what directions to take, where to get answers and so on. You are also programming the energetic grid with your intention to bring it all in and provide you with the physical manifestation of what you have asked for.

For now, I would like to invite you to take the plunge and dream big. Remember that whatever you come up with has three beneficiaries: First, *you* will benefit – it's your life! Second, others will benefit from what you achieve, create, build and contribute. And third, the world at large will benefit as well, both physically and energetically. And that is a *huge* deal.

You *matter*. And *your dreams count*.

Exercise: The Perfect Day

This is a very simple but extraordinarily powerful exercise for you to try. But it is one that I have done for years and give to all of my private coaching clients and group workshops.

Take three pages in your notebook and write what your perfect day would look like. What time would you get up? Who are you with? Where are you? What does your home look like? Who lives with you? Include all of the details you can think of.

Feel free to write a story about it. I have done this myself and you would be amazed at how good it feels and how much of it actually comes to fruition. The way I live my life now schedule-wise is what I always envisioned when I was back in a corporate-job schedule. I would write about it in my journal all the time. And now I get up as my body needs to and sometimes that is at 8am, sometimes 11am. I create my day as I go. And that works for me. I am much happier that way and much more creative.

Take the time to really play with this. And you can upgrade it as you go. Remember we are going to work backward from the big picture. So you do not have to worry about the 'how' right now. Just write.

The next step is to take a look at how you will feel when this comes to fruition. The feeling part is huge. This includes both your physical and emotional feelings.

So if you have a vision of waking up by the ocean, expound on how you will feel. Will you feel exhilarated, joyful, calm, expansive? What will the air smell like? What will the textures in your space feel like? Will you be able to just get up and walk down to the beach? Will the sand feel good under your feet? How warm is the water? Do you hear seagulls?

This process actually imprints the vision into your energetic grid and it is like turning on the ignition in the car. So go ahead and play with the vision now and when you are done we will get into developing the core tools that will help you bring it to fruition.

The Yeah Buts, the What Ifs and the If Onlys

So let me ask you how do you feel after completing the perfect day exercise? My hunch is that you may feel excited and joyful that you let the lid off and really went deep into exploration. But you also may be saying, "Yeah, but I can't do this because ..." or "What if this never happens?" or you may be feeling remorseful, like "If only I was younger or older or had more of this or that …" I am not going to delve deeply into these as it will just create drag in your energy. The solutions will unfold throughout the rest of our time together. But I will say this: Much of the anxiety that these questions carry is due to not having the missing pieces of your Energetic Communication System and a full understanding of how the collective consciousness and energetic grid work. As you gain access to these other pieces in Part II of the book, your doubt will decrease and your confidence will rise dramatically.

I also know that you may be feeling vulnerable, a bit nervous, even a bit angry that you have tried this before and it has not worked, or you don't know how to do it and you will be disappointed. Not to worry, we are going to tackle it all and you are going to realize you are so much further along than you think.

First, take a look at what you wrote. And realize that this is only a small indicator of the blessings that are available for you! Within this vision are all sorts of opportunities for you to make major contributions to yourself, to others and to the world at large. There are seeds planted there and if you let them grow you will be helping way more people than yourself!

Essentially, what you desire, desires you! Look at the word "de-sire"… "de" means "of"; "sire" means "the Father." Desire means "of the Father." All of your desires are heaven sent. So there is a way for you to achieve them or something even better.

Second, please understand that your logical mind and physical action alone cannot do it all. Your Aha! Factor is the key that will help you to know what directions to take, decisions to make, the timing of when to move forward and when to hold back, and all sorts of other guidance. I am going to teach you all about becoming fluent in the language of your Energetic Communication System in the next section so that you can operate with a full tank instead of on just a partial one. This will rapidly increase your success rate and how quickly things go for you.

Third, please be flexible with how things configure. As I have found so many times, what seems like a dead end turns out to be a shortcut. So as you visualize, just focus on the feelings, what it all looks like and why you really want it. Your Aha! Factor will accelerate your dreams and guide you step by step. And the energetic grid is the delivery truck for your dreams. So with these two extra tools you are in for a real treat. You will finally be plugged in and able to receive the information you need to move forward on all levels.

And when it comes to being in what many experts call "energetic alignment" or a "vibrational match" with your desires, you will finally be able to tangibly know what that looks like and how to get yourself there.

The Creative Engines

I have done thousands of intuitive readings for clients over the years and each morning I channel information from my guides in my journals, which I often share with my clients. I want to share a very interesting insight with you that was provided to me during a private intuitive session I was conducting. I think this will be very helpful to prepare us as we move into Part II, which goes into detail about how your Aha! Factor works.

The insight is that the Aha! Factor is most available to us when we are inspired.

When we allow ourselves to have a vision that we are inspired by and invested in, our intuition can come through loud and clear to assist us. So instead of succumbing to the negative voices inside that try to limit you to think about only what is within your immediate reach, take the all-important step to get clear on your vision.

If you find somewhere quiet and tune in to your Infinite Self, it will assist you in perceiving the biggest and best version of your life, with an incredible sense of knowing and inspiration. Then it will let you know the steps to take to go forward. Your Aha! Factor will then be operating at full capacity and the whole world, both energetic and physical, will come alive with the support, resources and people you need to fulfill your dreams!

PART II

ACTIVATE YOUR AHA! FACTOR TO ACCELERATE YOUR DREAMS

Chapter Eight

LEARNING THE LANGUAGE OF YOUR AHA! FACTOR

As we briefly discussed in Part I, your Energetic Communication System consists of five basic parts:

1. The intention you send or question you ask
2. The language of your intuition
3. The language of telepathy
4. The language of channeling
5. The integration of the energetic information with your physical action

When you regularly combine the use of these in your daily life, you start to see a steady stream of energetic communication and guidance that enables you to navigate your world with efficiency. You also gain much more ability to create what you truly want instead of appearing to be the victim of circumstance.

Now that we have covered the basics, we are going to embark on learning how to recognize and engage in each of these disciplines and how you can integrate them into your day. This will ensure that you establish a strong connection to guidance from your Infinite Self, as well as a flow of inspiration, resources, positive circumstances, helpful people and more.

When it comes to bringing our dreams to fruition, it is very easy to get lost in a sea of to-do lists and goal-setting plans. It is also easy to get overwhelmed by the challenge of how to bring it all into being. And many people give up before they even get started.

Before you throw in the towel or get worried that I am asking you to jump off of a high ledge, I want to share with you the often-hidden tools that you have built in, which can support you in actualizing your ideas in record time.

Wouldn't it make sense that if your dreams are so important not only to yourself but also to the world at large, that you would be provided with the tools and resources to support you, both in discovering what those dreams are and in making them come true as well? After all, when you are successful, everyone benefits.

We have a lot more power than we are aware of. And while we hear rumblings of things like "trust your gut instinct" or "follow your intuition," it is not usually a core skill set that anyone sets out to ensure that they master. In fact, we are often taught the complete opposite – to take pride in our ability to be logical and to follow our head rather than our heart.

But this approach could not be more misguided. Just as we have physical senses that help us navigate and function in our world, we also have an overlay of energetic senses that do so as well. Those senses are there to protect, guide and inspire us. But most importantly, our energetic senses are the link between our physical bodies and the greater version of ourselves. They keep us connected to our Infinite Selves, which is where all knowledge, wisdom, solutions, ideas and resources can be found. Your Infinite Self has access to absolutely everything and knows what is available, way beyond the capacities of what you perceive in the physical world.

As we learned in Part I, the language that the infinite version of you uses to stay connected and to provide you with all of the resources along the way is called your intuition. *We are all born with the language of our energetic communication system!* People often say to me, "Mari, you have a gift. You are so intuitive." And I quickly tell them that they have it too. We are all born with it. And the only difference between you and me is that I have taken the time to develop it to a professional level. Its just like we all brush our teeth, but a dentist can perform the big stuff, like the root canals and filling cavities.

How many times have you heard that we don't come with an owner's manual and we have to learn as we go? I am here to give you a manual on how to recognize and strengthen your intuition to be your most reliable tool for not only receiving clear inspiration, but also for getting support in attracting the right people and resources to support you. Your intuition will also enable you to know when someone is telling the truth or not, and it is your most reliable decision-making tool, because it is never wrong. Without training, you may interpret it wrong or not perceive it all, but once you understand how it works and the various ways to work with it, you will quickly come to lean on it more than ever.

What about Logic?

Does this mean that we are throwing out logic? Absolutely not! In fact logic is a partner to intuition. Logic is the second step after getting intuitive guidance because it is the part that puts what you have perceived into action. It is also the part that helps you to discern what the next steps are and to put everything into action in the physical world. Intuition without action does not get you very far. But logic without intuition gets you into a real mess as well, because it usually leads you down a rabbit hole of details that is loaded with unnecessary work, analysis and stress, all of which can cost you a lot of time, money and energy.

You may be wondering if this is hard to do. And it really isn't. You are already using all of the pieces, but may not be recognizing them. Once you know what you are looking at and how all the pieces fit together, you will be able to connect all of the dots and you will be on full operating power with consciousness of what you are doing. You will be amazed at how easy it is and how efficient it can be as well. When you let your Aha! Factor lead the way instead of your logical mind alone, things go forward so much more quickly!

Chapter Nine

THE ANATOMY OF AN
AHA! MOMENT

The first thing that we do prior to receiving any answer is to set an intention or ask a question. Whether we are aware of it or not, we are constantly asking questions in our minds and wondering how we can bring something to fruition or turn things around, if someone will behave this way or that way, how we will be able to get what we want, how can we get out of a tough situation and so on – the list goes on.

We also set intentions without meaning to by what we focus on and repeat in our thoughts, feelings and actions. So if we are constantly saying we are too fat or broke or never have enough, we are setting intentions to be overweight, short on cash and lacking resources. I always say, "Worry is negative prayer." And the way that worry reads on the energetic grid is as a repetitive loop of programming for the worst.

As you go through the remainder of this book, take the time to get very clear on what you really desire.

I suggest you write a list of the big things you desire and a list of the smaller day-to-day things as well. As you write you are setting intentions. And you are programming both your energetic grid and your Aha! Factor to start participating in the process to lead you to your goals.

It is important to choose what you desire and to be specific. But then you also need to be willing to have an even better outcome than what you have asked for. I have learned the hard way that being too specific can really limit you. And that not being specific enough can slow things down as well. Finding the balance takes practice and a bit of trial and error.

Once you set your intention you are ready to start receiving energetic guidance and you have turned on the switches of your energetic communication system.

One of the most common references to the existence of intuition that we have in modern times is what we call the "Aha! Moment." In my experience an Aha! Moment is the point where our physical consciousness intersects with a recognizable glimpse of our Infinite Self. It is an opening, a gateway in which we expand into a greater awareness and, like dropping a pebble into a still pond, our intuition drops an insight into our physical consciousness.

The 3 Steps to an Aha! Moment

There are three basic steps and when combined they create an Aha! Moment.

Step 1: Our four energetic centers, called the Four Clairs (clairvoyance, clairsentience, claircognizance and clairaudience), energetically let us know that we are receiving guidance. These may feel like déjà vu, a gut feeling, an instant knowing, lyrics playing in your head or an actual voice in your ear letting you know a particular piece of information.

Step 2: The energetic sense is followed up by a physical sensation in our bodies.

Step 3: The energetic and physical sensations we experience are then supported by signs, symbols and synchronicities appearing in our environment to reinforce the accuracy of our senses.

When these markers of communication happen, we feel the sensation of an Aha! Moment.

Step 1: The Four Clairs

As we have already established, at birth we are all provided with a set of four senses in addition to our five physical senses of taste, touch, smell, sight and hearing. These are called the Four Clairs. They consist of:

Clairvoyance: Spiritual Sight

Clairaudience: Spiritual Hearing

Clairsentience: Spiritual Feeling

Claircognizance: Spiritual Knowing

When we are children, these senses are fully functional and we use them naturally. For example, when kids have imaginary friends, they are honing their channeling abilities and their capacity to receive guidance and strength from energetic beings beyond their logical mind. After a certain age this is no longer considered to be appropriate. These senses are present and available to us, but we generally ignore them. I am not saying that we should have imaginary friends as adults, but our guides and angels are with us for our entire life, not just in childhood. By bringing a childlike wonder and openness into our work with our guides, we continue the natural progression of our inborn energetic communication skills, which are often lost in adult life and then later have to be relearned, usually when a crisis hits and we have nowhere else to turn.

Most children are very aware of their Four Clairs and actively use them through the spontaneous expression of their emotions and imagination – until their parents reason them away from using their intuition, convincing them to rely on logic and intellect, which by themselves are never as accurate as the internal voice of inspired action from their Infinite Selves.

These four spiritual senses are just as real as your senses of smell, touch, taste, sight or hearing. When we deliberately and consistently identify, develop and incorporate the Four Clairs into our daily lives, we are completely open and able to receive the full answers to our prayers and intentions. Our spiritual activities are much more powerful and become effortless as we eliminate the strain of wondering how and if our prayers are being heard and answered.

Contrary to popular belief, psychics, mediums, prophets and spiritual intuitives have not been given "special" gifts; they've only developed the senses which most of us are unaware of and do not yet embrace. The Four Clairs are available to everyone and once we become aware of each of them, we can open the gateway to harnessing and relying on them as we do all of our physical senses.

When choosing to open the Four Clairs, it is first important to identify which of the four you are most naturally using already.

How to identify clairvoyance

Many people have vivid dreams that either come true or provide answers. Perhaps you have daydreams of loved ones that later are confirmed as true. This is clairvoyance or spiritual seeing. People who are clairvoyant are generally very visual by nature. If you asked a natural clairvoyant what they most enjoyed about a movie when leaving the theater, they would be able to speak vividly about the cinematography, the sets or the vase on the table behind the main character.

How to identify clairaudience

Those with clairaudience as their core sense are more likely to hear guidance in their dominant ear. Right-handed people may hear in their right ear first and vice versa for lefties. Clairaudients tend to enjoy music, can hear details that others ignore; when coming out of a movie, they will be able to tell you a great deal about the soundtrack or specific lines in the script.

How to identify clairsentience

Clairsentient people feel thoughts and energy through what most call the "pit of their stomach," but it is actually their solar plexus, the area right above the navel in the center of the body. For example, mothers often say they feel their "mother's intuition" right in this area.

Clairsentient people tend to be able to feel the energy of a person. They will often say, "This just does not feel right to me," or "The energy feels really good around this idea." If you asked a clairsentient-dominant person about what they thought of a movie, they would most probably tell you about how they felt and their perception of the relationships and the feelings that were emoted by the characters during the story.

How to identify claircognizance

Claircognizant-dominant people tend to know things way beyond their area of expertise. Spiritual knowing transcends practical learning. Many times, claircognizant people are mistakenly labeled as "know-it-alls." What is different, though, is that they are usually right!

Someone with claircognizance as their dominant spiritual sense can often tell a person how to do something without ever having done it themselves. When leaving the movie theater, a claircognizant person will likely say, "I knew the ending all along. I knew that the lead character would return to save the baby at the end of the movie."

Once you have identified your dominant Clair and you have a general sense of the others, you can begin to work on developing the other Clairs to be just as reliable for you as your physical senses. As you develop your trust in your spiritual receptive centers to provide guidance to you, you will be able to receive consistent and accurate information that will greatly assist you in both your daily and major life decisions!

Step 2: Your Physical Body Responds and Reinforces Your Energetic Senses

It is very easy to think that your body doesn't have much to do with all of this energy stuff we are discussing. However, your body plays an integral part in the equation. It is one of the three legs that hold up the stool. Your body is the physical messenger of your intuition.

This is fascinating because your body is your psychic antenna that works hand in hand with your Four Clairs to reinforce that a message has just been transmitted to you energetically. This second step always happens right alongside of the energetic sensation. It is like an alarm that goes off, letting you know that you have mail.

There are a variety of physical signs that can occur to let you know that your intuition is communicating with you. In general you will find that when you ask a question or receive an answer or an intuitive hit, you will get a feeling of lightness for yes or heaviness for no. But it goes much deeper than that. And it is often a bit hard to detect a light or heavy feeling if you are emotionally attached to a particular outcome. So let's go over some of the physiological signs that your body sends to you to let you know something is up.

Getting goose bumps, or as I like to call them, "truth bumps," is a very common sign. This sensation is a tell-tale indication that you should pay attention and in most cases it is a yes answer or a sign of truth.

Feeling a chill is also a strong physical sign. This can be either positive or negative depending on the situation. The way to know is to see what other signs you are receiving. For example, if you get a chill and a feeling of lightness or a lift in mood, it is positive. A speeding up of your heartbeat or a sensation of butterflies in your stomach, with a light, happy child-like feeling, can be a positive sign as well.

If, however, you get a chill and it reads more like a cold eerie shiver and a dropping feeling then the sign is probably negative. Also, a slight feeling of nausea, lightheadedness or dizziness can be a negative sign or mean that the answer is no. Sweaty palms or a flash of heat can also be a sign that something is not right. I am not talking about a full-blown menopausal hot flash here. It is just a quick sensation that comes and goes rapidly. So please don't get concerned if you are going through hormonal changes and get hot flashes. These are two different things!

Your body is very in tune with your intuition and has strong energetic receptors built in. So it won't steer you wrong. And when you start to practice by taking note both of your Clairs and how your body feels, you will be amazed at how quickly you will become fluent in interpreting your intuition. The more you pay attention, the more you will get back. Your intuition, and the greater consciousness that we all tap into is switched on 24/7. It is like a current that runs in a way similar to the figures of the stocks that run across the lower third of the screen on the popular news and finance channels. This current is always on, waiting for you to tune in. And when you do, both your energetic and physical senses perceive and broadcast it for you.

Now let's move on to the third step: your environment.

Step 3: Your Intuition Uses Signs, Symbols and Synchronicity

This is where the fun starts, because now your intuition brings you even greater signs that can be very specific and quite special. When your intuition teams up with the energetic grid, it aligns with signs, symbols and synchronized experiences to let you know the answers to your questions, provide you with guidance, the next steps, inspiration, protection and much more.

As you learn to interpret these signs, you will realize that all the world whispers and there is always some sort of message waiting for you. These can be both great and small. Often they are funny or even miraculous.

One sign that I often see is angel feathers in strange places. For example, I was actually quite tired today and knew that I needed to come to the bookstore to work on this chapter. I procrastinated for hours, but I am a night person and do much better when I wait for my natural energy cycles to kick in and follow those. After a lot of talking on the phone, internet surfing and other good old-fashioned procrastination that goes hand in hand with the creative process, I finally hunkered down at my favorite table in the café and got to work. As I started typing, I felt a bit of a chill and I looked up to see a white feather floating right above eye level. I say a prayer before I start a writing session, to call in my muses and angels, and that was their way of letting me know that I was not alone and thanking me for hunkering down and getting to work. I laughed and kept typing, knowing that somehow, someway they got me back to the chair and the computer and that it would be a good session. I even exceeded my daily page goal by several thousand words, so that was a cool bonus, too. This happens when you "follow the energy" and listen to your intuition. Could I have come to my writing space earlier in the day? Yes. Would I have been as productive? No.

So let's get you going on how to recognize and interpret the signs, symbols and synchronicities in your world and kick your intuition into high gear!

Signs, symbols and synchronicities

How will your Infinite Self communicate with you through your environment and other people via your intuition? As we discussed earlier, your intuition will always use the Four Clairs to communicate your inspired action first. Firstly, you will get a feeling, have a flash of a vision, hear a thought or have a strong sense of knowing. Secondly, you will then get a physical sensation such as a feeling of lightness, a cool chill, goosebumps, a flash of heat or a sense of heaviness.

Then the third thing your intuition will do is to take this further into your environment and employ other signs, symbols, and synchronicities (occurrences that seem like "coincidences") to get the point across and provide you with hope, inspiration and wonder as you marvel at the power of miracles and manifestation! It will also use these to provide you with specific information about what to do next, how to do things and who to get in touch with.

Sometimes, your intuition will use your environment or circumstances because you are not listening to it and acting on it from your Four Clairs. When we become frightened or feel unsure about what to do, we procrastinate or ignore the signs that we are getting. So, in order to get the point across, the signs get stronger and stronger.

If you ignore the inspired action, the signs may get more severe and repetitive.

Examples of this are when people lose their jobs, or get a divorce or have a severe illness. In most cases, there were tiny signs that got bigger and bigger until they finally reached a crisis level and got them to pay attention.

But, on a more positive note, your Aha! Factor loves to combine wonderful signs, symbols and synchronicities to excite and inspire you to take action with emotion, urgency and passion! Inspiration and passion are the octane of manifestation. When you infuse your action with good positive emotion, wonder and joy, amazing miracles can truly happen. Answered prayer is much easier to receive when you take *inspired action*. It is a win–win for both you and your Infinite Self!

What to look for

My motto is: Don't look for anything, but be aware of what is a significant sign.

What I mean by this is if you are just staring out into the universe looking for signs, you will see them everywhere and they will not come with that special punch of spontaneity that is truly magical and Divinely guided. I have had clients who would constantly tell me of sign after sign and yet they would not move forward with action. This is a pitfall of constantly watching for signs!

Engage Your Four Clairs to Interpret the Validity of Signs

It can be very tempting to spend a ton of time looking for signs. However, I suggest that instead of compulsively sign-watching, it's better to focus in on what your Four Clairs are telling you. When you see something that seems like a sign, first go into your Four Clairs and ask yourself:

- Does the sign invoke a feeling of knowing? (claircognizance)
- Do you feel a strong emotional feeling? (clairsentience)
- Does it feel like déjà vu? (clairvoyance)
- Or, perhaps it sounds right, like something you have heard before (clairaudience).

Also take notice of the physical sensation when you get a sign. Do you feel a cool or warm sensation in your body? Do you get the goosebumps or a flash of heat? Do you sense a feeling of lightness or heaviness?

Be Open to Receiving and Responding to Inspired Action

Inspired action always comes with a good strong sense of urgency. Now I don't mean a "freaking-out-chicken-without-a-head" panic! When I say urgency, I mean a strong knowing that it is the absolute right action to take. You may feel like, "I don't know why I feel this, but I have to follow it and do it … now."

Resignation versus Resolution

Resignation, or a feeling that this is the "only way, the last hope, I have no choice" and so on stems from a feeling of disempowerment and usually happens when you have procrastinated and ignored signs and now have backed yourself into a corner. Resignation is never what your Infinite Self wants from you, or for you!

Inspired action will always come as a feeling of empowerment and resolution, not resignation! When your Infinite Self is sending you inspiration, you will feel a sense of resolve, a knowing that it is just the right thing to do at this time. It may not be the easiest thing. It may require you to feel vulnerable or take you out of your comfort zone but you will also feel a sense of peace that this hunch is truly a sign of inspired action. Because, in addition to the sign, you will get back-up from the Four Clairs. It may not be all four Clairs, but you will get the extra punch of energy from them as it is needed.

What to Do When You Get the Signs

First, say thank you to your Infinite Self. Gratitude always fuels a rapid stream of more inspiration. Second, if necessary, take action immediately. Remember, your Infinite Self can and will only release the next step to you once you have taken the first one that you've been given. Third, *write it down*. If it is just a sign of hope, or a specific action, keep a record of it.

Recording the signs and synchronicities gives you three things:

1. You will feel encouraged as you collect the signs.

2. The combination of signs gives you a greater meaning and message as they unfold. Sometimes, they reveal timing or changes to be made. Sometimes, the signs will take you on a tangent where healing or resolution of obstacles is needed before you can receive guidance.

3. Your Infinite Self is always giving you a creation "blueprint" so that you know how to repeat it in the future.

Chapter Ten

ALL THE WORLD WHISPERS: 101 SPIRITUAL SIGNS, SYMBOLS AND SYNCHRONICITIES

The following is a list of 101 positive signs of inspiration that I have received and recorded myself. Sometimes, the signs are just warm, fuzzy reminders that you are not alone. And many times the signs are directions to take inspired actions that will push you out of your comfort zone.

Remember that in order to invoke change, you must be willing to let go of old patterns that no longer serve you and take what I like to call the "inspired risk" of new actions.

These are a small sample of how your Infinite Self can and will communicate with you when you open your heart and mind to receive. Use the list as a point of reference to get you started, and be sure to add signs and guidance that you receive on your own.

Signs Showing Your Aha! Factor Is Tuned in and Turned on

Visions

1. Seeing rainbows anywhere – especially when you are seeking reassurance that things will get better

2. Seeing ladybugs – good luck and wishes are coming true

3. Seeing dragonflies – joy and light (symbols of the fairies)

4. Seeing hawks – you will be receiving important messages from your Infinite Self, so pay attention!

5. Finding coins and pennies – abundance and money are coming your way

6. Seeing license plates with a message

7. Seeing billboards with positive messages or sayings that apply to your concerns

8. Seeing magazine articles, TV interviews or shows at unusual times about issues or concerns that you are dealing with

9 Seeing pictures, statues or symbols of fairies in unusual places

10 Seeing pictures, statues or symbols of angels in unusual places

11 Seeing spiders – creative juices are available and flowing

12 Seeing grasshoppers – leaps of joy

13 Seeing crickets – extremely good luck

14 Seeing lightning bugs (fireflies) – extremely good luck, especially in love

15 Seeing angel-shaped cloud formations in the sky – you are protected and to have hope

16 Seeing an owl – the goddess Athena, who symbolizes wisdom and empowerment

17 Seeing a red fox – magic is in the air and very good luck

18 Seeing doves of all types – peaceful outcomes, especially in love and relationships

Seeing butterflies – positive transformation is taking place for you

Seeing baby animals of all kinds symbolizes birth, renewal and the inspiration of a fresh start

 Seeing website banner ads that have sayings applicable to your concerns

 Seeing or smelling orchids – a sign of passion or love

Seeing the word "love" anywhere

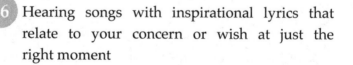 Seeing the words "joy," "harmony" or "peace" repetitively

Seeing a blooming lotus flower in a pond

Sounds

Hearing songs with inspirational lyrics that relate to your concern or wish at just the right moment

 Hearing of a book that addresses your concerns

Scents

 Smelling the scent of flowers when there are none nearby

Smelling rose scent – very powerful and significant as it represents the highest Divine love

Smelling the scent of a loved one's cologne when they are not there

Discovery

 Finding feathers in unusual places – angels are nearby

Finding flowers in unusual places, as if they were left for you

Finding the initials of loved ones in unusual places

Finding heart-shaped stones on the beach or out in nature – promise of love and happy romance. (I have found over 100!)

 Finding heart-shaped shells

36 Finding crystals and researching their meaning

37 Finding rocks with a natural hole bored all the way through them – these are said to be holy stones that can be used for good luck and protection

38 Finding something on sale that you needed and were not yet looking for

39 Finding mushrooms in your lawn or garden – according to folklore this is very good luck and the fairies have taken up residence!

40 Listening to children's conversations that seem to be effortless and prophetic in their wisdom

41 Stumbling onto a website that answers your questions

Intuitive Thoughts

42 Feeling led to send a book, CD or website to a friend in need of inspiration – just because. This is how your Infinite Self uses you to send inspiration to others

43 Choosing to listen to the voice of your heart instead of the voice of your inner critic

44 Choosing to have faith instead of fear … just for today …

45 Choosing to absolve someone, who you know was wrong, from blame and guilt and release it to surrender and faith in order to free up *your* own energy to receive even better

46 Forgiving yourself for your personal mistakes and shortcomings

47 Choosing to let go and forgive even when you know the other person is guilty of hurting you

The Kindness of Strangers

48 Having a total stranger looking you in the eye and smiling without saying a word

49 Receiving unexpected help from someone

50 Getting your coffee or tea for free from the barista at your favorite coffee shop

51 Being offered chocolate – it soothes a broken heart

Numbers

52 Seeing repetitive number sequences in various places (See Dr. Doreen Virtue's book *Angel Numbers* – a must-have for your spiritual library)

53 Seeing the numbers 111 – energetic gateways are opening for you, your thoughts are manifesting

54 Seeing 222 – keep the faith, everything will be fine

55 Seeing 333 – you have connected and merged with the highest of spirit guides and they are working with you now

56 Seeing 444 – you are surrounded by angels who are helping you

57 Seeing 555 – positive transition and change are taking place – let go and allow it

58 Seeing 666 – focus on spirit to balance and heal

59 Seeing 777 – rewards are yours now

60 Seeing 888 – abundance and prosperity are here for you now

61 Seeing 999 – it's time to get to work on your spiritual path without delay! Move, move, move!

Inspired Actions

62 Feeling compelled to let a bug or a rodent live by moving it outside instead of killing it, honoring its life force within

63 Lighting candles that burn clean and clear – for example, you can try pink for love, green for money, and white for guidance and protection. There are books and charts available online showing all of the different colors and their meanings

64 Receiving phone calls, text messages or emails from someone you were recently thinking about

65 Feeling compelled to feed the wildlife in your backyard (garden) including the birds, squirrels, other creatures and insects

66 When a book falls off the shelf in front of you – your Infinite Self is providing you with new knowledge

67 Making a "wrong" turn that leads you to a sign of encouragement you would not have otherwise seen

68 Having a conversation with someone and they mention a book or a subject that you were thinking about or need information about

69 Hearing about the same book, movie or person three times

70 Choosing the same angel or other guidance card from an oracle deck randomly, multiple times

71 Turning on a movie just when a particular line of dialogue applies to your situation

72 Feeling inspired to go into a church or other house of worship that does not have a service in session and finding the door open

73 Feeling compelled to light a candle for inspiration

74 Getting to a destination late and finding that everyone else was late as well

75 Feeling compelled to look up an old friend and finding them. This is usually your Infinite Self

inspiring you to clear the past or rekindle a friendship in a new space and time.

76 Feeling compelled to rescue a plant on the clearance rack of a home and garden store

77 Feeling inspired to volunteer for a good cause, especially involving kids or animals

78 Feeling compelled to pick up litter or trash as you walk in the park or at the beach

79 Having the time to do something special due to unexpected bad weather that prevents you from leaving the house

80 Feeling led to start a journal or a diary – your Infinite Self loves the opportunity for this type of direct communication!

81 Picking up a book, closing your eyes and asking, "What is most important for me to know right now?" – then opening the page to just the right information

82 Feeling inspired to pick up the phone and be the first one to apologize

83 Feeling compelled to step out of your comfort zone and respond to conflict differently than you normally would

84 Feeling compelled to step out of your comfort zone and respond to fear differently than you normally would

85 Feeling compelled to step out of your comfort zone and respond to anger differently than you normally would

86 Feeling compelled to allow yourself to be a work in progress, even if it's just for today

87 Feeling led to stop spooking yourself with "worst case scenario" thoughts and catastrophic thinking

88 Feeling compelled to send thanks to all parts of your body – the energy of your Infinite Self resides in every cell of the body. Love them all

89 Feeling compelled to do art of any kind

90 Feeling compelled to write poetry or lyrics of any kind

91 Feeling compelled to do gardening of any kind

Feeling compelled to dance or do exercise of any kind

93 Feeling compelled to stop and take a deep breath – intuitive information travels on the molecules of oxygen that we take in. The more you breathe deeply, the clearer the information gets

94 Feeling compelled to sit quietly in meditation of any kind for any length of time

95 Feeling compelled to keep fresh flowers in your home or office

96 Feeling compelled to say thank you silently to all of the people you see

97 Feeling compelled to say thank you silently to all the objects you use, recognizing the energy that is present in all things

98 Feeling compelled to speak your truth, even when you are afraid that the consequences may anger the other person, or cause them to reject or fire you

99 Feeling compelled to choose silence instead of speaking in order to allow someone else their

free will. Silence in many cases is much stronger than speaking

 Feeling compelled to say "I love you" to anyone or anything

 Witnessing a series of similar signs on different days or in different places

Chapter Eleven

TELEPATHY AND YOUR
AHA! FACTOR

Now that we have learned the mechanics of setting intention, how our intuition works and the anatomy of the Aha! Moment, it is time to learn about the next part of our Energetic Communication System – telepathy.

One of the least talked-about parts of our Energetic Communication System is that of telepathy – the ability to communicate by non-verbally sending and receiving pictures, words, a request, a longing, even a song to another person by our focused thoughts or energy.

Telepathy is a combination of energy and intention that engages your intuitive senses – the Four Clairs that we discussed in the previous chapter – and our use of the energetic grid to focus and transfer thoughts, feelings and emotions to others. We can also receive telepathic messages and often do so without attributing it to this energetic ability.

If you think carefully I am sure you will be able to find times when you communicated telepathically with someone. Have you ever been thinking about a person and they just call you up on the phone, out of the blue? Or thought of something that you needed from the store, but were too busy to get and your spouse came home with it after work saying, "I don't know why but something just told me to get it"? Have you ever walked into a room and could feel someone was angry with you or had been talking badly about you and later found out that it was true? Have you ever thought of your pet when they are on the other side of the house and seemingly out of nowhere they came into the room where you were, seeking attention. And has anyone ever said "Oh, your ears must have been burning – we were just talking about you!"

These are all examples of your telepathic abilities in action. This part of our Energetic Communication System proves that we share thoughts on our energetic grid of creation even when we don't verbalize them. And these thoughts can happen from thousands of miles away. We are all connected and once you realize this personal power you can expand your ability to send and receive information more powerfully than you can imagine.

Let's take a look at a few of the ways that you can deliberately work with your telepathic abilities. Many years ago I used to teach intuitive classes for children. I was hired by moms to come over after school and teach their kids how to work with energy and engage their natural intuitive abilities. Kids are fantastic at this because they do not need to intellectualize, criticize, judge or mentally understand the mechanics of what they are learning before they will give it a try. This is completely opposite to the way adults learn.

One of the games we would play was for the brother, who I will call Bobby, and his sister Sally to send each other messages through their thoughts. First I would have them sit cross-legged with their backs to each other. I would give Bobby a picture of a piece of fruit and instruct him to silently call out the fruit in the picture in his head to Sally. I said to envision that he was seeing Sally across the room and was holding a real piece of fruit in front of her. He was then to silently call it out to her over and over in his head without saying a word verbally.

I instructed Sally to just say the very first vision that came into her head. In the beginning stages of the game I would ask, "Is Bobby sending you an apple, a pear, a blueberry or a banana?" so she could choose from a narrowed-down field of options. I also let Bobby know that if he wanted to send an even stronger message in addition to silently saying the name of the fruit, he could also envision eating it, and send the sense of what it tasted, smelled and felt like to his sister with his thoughts.

Bobby and Sally were both incredibly good at sending and receiving their images and had a ball trading messages. This is a fantastic way to boost accurate telepathic communication, as anything that engages more than one of the senses, whether verbally or non-verbally, is always easier to perceive. Another variation is to give pieces of real fruit to the person sending to hold, so they can engage themselves in the details of it while silently sending their experience to their partner.

As we moved forward with the game, we moved one kid across the room so they were no longer touching and the results were still great. Then they went in to two separate rooms and still were able to send and receive messages at the same success rate. They had such a good time and so did I!

Now while we play this as a game, developing your own telepathic skills is an extremely powerful life tool. The kids started to send each other messages in school. One day Bobby had a stomach ache and Sally was able to receive his message that he was not feeling well. Sure enough, when Bobby was not outside for recess (breaktime), Sally went to the school nurse to find him there. While not the best of circumstances, this incident built even more trust and faith for Bobby and Sally in their telepathic abilities and, in conjunction with their physical senses, having their energetic senses in gear was a super power boost for their wellbeing, safety, overall confidence and self-esteem.

Can you imagine how powerful you would feel if you could truly lean on and trust your own Energetic

Communication System like this? You can give this a try with your friends, using more adult topics or real-life scenarios. This is great to use in relationships with people you are close to and in reality you already do. How many times have you heard two lovers say "Oh I just love him, we finish off each other's sentences and say the same thing at the same time without the other one knowing. It's amazing!"

Once you ignite, start working with and using your telepathic ability, be sure to use your intuitive skills to check out what you perceive from your telepathy. For example, when you get a hunch (or as we say in the business an "energetic hit") check for its validity with your Four Clairs. What are you sensing? Are you getting a vision, hearing a word in your head, getting a feeling? Are you receiving just a strong knowing of what the message is? Now check in with your body. Are you getting "truth bumps," a whoosh feeling, a bit of a chill or butterflies? How about signs, symbols and synchronicities? Anything coming up that feels like it is validating your perceptions?

This is how you are engaging your Aha! Factor to manage your energetic perceptions right alongside your physical senses. And your logic is what reminds you of the pieces you should be looking for to evaluate if your perception is valid.

Can you see how it all works hand in hand? Here's to the Aha! Moments that I am sure you will have!

Telepathy can be used with animals, too. Animals communicate with us telepathically all of the time. As an animal communicator I have been able to perceive what my pets desire and also the stories of other animals, such as those in shelters, by their telepathic accounts of what happened to them.

My Maine Coone cat, Tinkerbell, who I adopted when she was four, is usually quite outgoing with women and people she knows. But whenever a man came to my home, she would run and hide. It became clear to me that she was having some issues, bad memories or flashbacks. During one of my meditations I telepathically asked her why she was so frightened. And she sent me a vision of her when she was in the shelter. She showed that before she was adopted she lived in several foster homes and that when she was in that system a man would always come to pick her up and take her back to a cage in the shelter or pet store to be seen for possible adoption. She was always afraid that she would end up in the shelter where animals are put to sleep. So when men came to my house she would run and hide for a bit to make sure that they were not coming to take her away.

This made so much sense to me. I told her telepathically that she was in her forever home and that she never had to worry about that again. I told her both verbally and through pictures. I showed her visions of us having company and the humans being very friendly to her and giving her treats, petting her kindly and then leaving the house without taking her with them. I showed her pictures in my mind of her being able to curl up with my other two cats, who are her best buddies and that all was well. It took a few times, but she no longer runs and hides like she used to. And if she does, it's for two minutes instead of two hours.

Telepathy is great to use when you are traveling and your animals are without you. You can speak to them by sending pictures, images in your head of reuniting with them. One thing that I do before leaving town is to tell them how many sunrises and sunsets that I will be gone for. This is the language that they understand and it really works quite well. When I come home they are calm and peaceful, not traumatized and needy.

So now it is time for you to start working with your own telepathic abilities. The best way to get great results is to practice a lot. Have fun with it. Send messages to your partner, friends, kids, family members, even to your colleagues and see what happens. Remember, the more feeling and emotion you can send with your images, the easier the message will be to perceive and receive.

Can Telepathy Work Against You?

The answer to this question is yes! I particularly see telepathic messages work against people in romantic relationships or situations where they have a romantic interest in someone. As with intuition, we are all born with built-in telepathy. Our most dominant and repetitive thoughts go out onto the energetic grid and the more emotion, feelings and attachments that we have, the more powerful the message is.

When women and men obsess on their significant other or someone that they are interested in, they can become what is perceived as energetically needy. This pushes the person away and jams up communications.

I have had so many clients call me for readings and say, "Mari, I haven't done anything. I haven't called or texted and I still don't hear from him!" I always ask, "Are you obsessing or perseverating on this? Are you thinking of every reason why this could be happening – constantly checking the phone, emails, his social media accounts?" When they say yes, even to just one or two of these things, and then explain that he doesn't know that they are doing that since he is not in contact, I always say, "Oh yes he does! Your energy is screaming at him!"

I suggest that they go and get distracted, date someone else, get a hobby or genuinely change gears and often they will hear from that person again. Why? Because the telepathic panic has ended. The void of energy being sent their way now says "I have moved on." And if you meant anything to that person, they will reach out.

Attachments can happen energetically and can be even more powerful than physical attachments. The more focus you put on someone, especially with high emotion, the more they feel it and this can make them run in the other direction. If an energetic attachment is happening in one of your relationships, the best thing to do is to let go, not just by not calling or texting, but also by shifting your thoughts, feelings and emotions to other topics. Literally unplug energetically and in most cases the person will reach out to you of their own accord. Why? Because they feel the energetic distance and freedom from the needy cords that were previously attaching you to them.

This tactic usually works like a charm. But it will not work if you do it for an hour or for two days and then start obsessing again! Give it two to six months and truly focus elsewhere. This is extremely healthy for any relationship in which you or your partner is feeling energetically claustrophobic.

Cool stuff, right? Now that you have the basics on how you can speak with people and animals who are alive and well in the physical world, in the next chapter we are going to move on to how to communicate energetically with those beings who are not embodied, such as angels, guides, crossed-over loved ones and your own Infinite Self. They are all available to you 24/7 with your third built-in energetic ability – channeling.

Chapter Twelve

CHANNELING:
A TWO-WAY CONVERSATION

Now we move on to one of the most exciting and often misunderstood abilities within your Energetic Communication System, the art of channeling. Sounds complicated, right? It is much simpler than you might think. Channeling is the ability to tap into specific energies and both perceive and send communications via what we call streams of consciousness.

Essentially you are capable of communicating and receiving full sentences and two-way conversations with other beings that are not in physical bodies, including your own Infinite Self. This is huge and very real. This part of the Energetic Communication System has been around since the beginning of time and evidence of it can be found in almost all cultures throughout history.

You may think that your ability to channel a download of guidance or to have a two-way conversation with your guides is highly unlikely or something that is best left to people like Esther

Hicks, the world-renowned channel of Abraham; J. Z. Knight the famous channel of Ramtha; or Lee Carroll, international channel of Kryon. While these are three of the top trance channels in the world, your innate channeling ability that is a part of your Energetic Communication System is not reliant in any way on you being able to go into a full-on trance and speak with a different accent about all sorts of world and galactic events. While this, of course, can be part of the most advanced versions of channeling – sort of equivalent to the Olympic level – that is not what I am referring to for our purposes of daily personal use.

Instead, we are going to focus on how you can get beyond small signs and guide posts and tap into full-on streams of consciousness that give you step-by-step guidance, wisdom and support on anything and everything that matters to you. You can tap into these streams of consciousness to help yourself creatively as well. I have channeled huge portions of this book. When I call in my channeling guides and then allow the thoughts to flow, I can download a huge amount of information in one sitting.

I channeled the last chapter in a 30-page handwritten stream of consciousness by simply asking my guides and writing muses to provide me with the information that you needed the most about telepathy. I asked for what would be relevant and easy for you to understand and inspiring for you to take action on.

After a walk out in nature – for me, the beach – and a big cup of tea, I sat down at my writing table, said my opening prayer and just started to write. I did not have an outline or points I wanted to cover. I just wrote the thoughts as they poured into my mind. And before I knew it, I had penned 30 handwritten pages.

When you engage with your guides it feels as if time stands still. It physically felt like I had been writing for 15 minutes, but when I looked at the clock I had spent an hour and 20 minutes. It all made sense. I felt good about that download and moved on to this one.

Channeling can be used for getting information about all aspects of your life both great and small. I have used it for coming up with new products, teaching my classes, guiding my clients, giving advice to friends and getting guidance on all sorts of issues in my personal life. I have also channeled guided messages from loved ones and celebrities who have crossed over. They may no longer be embodied, but their energy is still available to communicate and contribute to you.

The channeling ability, while not particularly well known, is present with inventors, scientists, athletes, musicians and many other creative types who create "new, never-been-seen-or-heard-before information." This original content is transferred from multi-dimensional worlds that are more advanced than us and is how we keep from blowing ourselves up or from being wiped out in epidemics.

When a particular challenge happens in society like AIDS or the drought in California or the need to evolve our transportation systems and so on, many members of the human race begin to long for a solution, a cure, a new invention. That enormous focus – the repetitive intention of "We need a cure now. Our loved ones are dying en masse!" coupled with intense emotion – opens the gateways on the energetic grid and gives permission to those who are capable to send solutions. Remember that grid of energy extends through all directions of time, all dimensions, all worlds, all planets and all life forms. That grid is alive and never turns off. So when an individual, a group or whole societies send out a cry, it is heard and responded to. Those who are trained to perceive and receive or create a solution are provided with a glimpse, a hypothesis, a moment of "Hmmm, what if we tried this?" And then they open up to the stream of consciousness. Usually that starts with an Aha! Moment and then moves into a download of steps to try and the solutions take form.

The solution evolves because the person puts in place the physical action plan to execute the energetic messages they received, often not knowing how they got the idea, but now knowing how to proceed.

How many times has something like this happened to you? Maybe not finding a cure for an epidemic or building a new spacecraft, but for everyday things such as solving a business problem at work, figuring out how to improve a recipe, sorting out a stubborn computer glitch or finding a successful way to communicate guidance to your teenager that they embrace and accept?

These solutions that feel like a flow, a knowing – an Aha! Moment – are very different from the arduous task of "figuring things out" that stems from the mind when it is not energetically engaged. When we are aware of and begin to allow the support of our built-in ability to channel, we realize that anything is possible, because we do not have to come up with it all by ourselves. Instead we can tap into the God of your understanding, our guides, the grid or a myriad of other energies that are always available.

I remember when I started my radio show, I was absolutely terrified. My logical mind got the best of me. So did my fear of sounding stupid, potentially running out of things to say and all sorts of other anxiety-driven worries. I wrote 30 pages of notes for that very first show! I was not in channeling mode at all, even though I had already been a professional-level channel for many years. I was operating totally from my logical mind and letting my fears drive me crazy with doubt. When I got on the phone with my producer, Sam, I was a babbling mess. He said, in his irreverent way, "Dude, you got this. Just breathe, put the notes away and flow with it." That one sentence and a big, deep breath clicked me over into channeling mode and off I went to do my first hour-long show without a hitch.

Now, three years later, I write a few bullet points a few minutes before the show and allow the stream of consciousness to speak through me. Why? Because that stream of consciousness is from the collective guides who also read the energy of every single person listening to the show or who will listen to the replays and podcasts at a later date. It guides me to include what the listeners need the most without me necessarily being mentally aware of it.

So how can you get started with plugging into your channeling ability and begin tapping into the stream of consciousness that is available to you? One of the easiest ways is to work with your journal and automatic writing. If you are more auditory, you may want to try this with a digital recorder instead of a notebook.

I personally started doing automatic writing when my fiancé passed away. I was so despondent. He was extremely spiritual and energetically advanced when he was alive, so I knew that he would come through if I gave the journaling a try. And after I learned the very easy basics of how to tap into the stream of consciousness, I would sit and write 10 or 20 pages of conversation, often interview style, where I would write one question as my own voice and then would pen the answers from him that I perceived.

Once I got comfortable with that and began learning about all of the various angels, guides and other energies available to communicate with in this way, I had great fun writing with them. It accelerated my career and many of the other things I was doing, tremendously. If I was dancing and trying to sort out a timing problem, I would channel my guides for that. When I was negotiating a business deal I would channel guidance from a different guide for that. The possibilities are endless. And if you can get out of your own way you will see that this can work wonders for you as well.

It is important to note that if you take the time to get good at becoming fluent in your intuition and practice your telepathy often so that you really grow to trust it, channeling will be much easier because you will be able to discern what is true guidance and what is actually your own mind.

In my Open to Channel courses, the biggest challenge for students is their ability to perceive the guidance and trust it. This is usually because they skipped over mastering their intuitive abilities first, and are not practicing on a regular basis to make it become a natural process. So please be sure to work diligently and consistently at always noticing the energetic aspects of all of your physical actions and plans. The practice has a cumulative effect. The more you focus, the more information you get. It is as simple as that!

While channeling can become quite a detailed process, if you practice the intuitive work such as telepathy and regular energetic hygiene, including personal clearing, energy work and so on, so that things are nice and clear, you will have an easy time getting the connection that you seek.

Can you have a two-way conversation with your guides and Infinite Self? The answer is yes! Here is the best exercise to use to get started. Once this becomes consistent for you, you will have a reliable tool to have a two-way conversation with your guides and be ready to move on to more advanced methods. (You can check out our website at www.TheAhaWay.com to learn more about our channeling and advanced channeling courses.)

After all, it is in the best interest of everyone for you to get the messages and answers to your prayers as quickly as possible! And your Infinite Self makes every attempt to give you answers that are as concrete as possible. The most important key is that you are consistent and open to listen, as well as that you are willing to accept them.

As we have discussed, you will see that your Infinite Self will send you verbal and written messages in the form of song lyrics, articles, TV shows and interviews, movies, bumper stickers, billboards, license plates, conversations with friends, overhearing conversations of strangers and in many other ways. But there is also a way to get messages that are much more personalized specifically to you.

I shared earlier that I discovered the amazing benefits and power of automatic writing after my fiancé passed away. It was amazing how I could continue to communicate with him energetically and it also opened up a whole new world of accessing information from the greater consciousness, my own angels and spirit guides.

If you are ready to receive written messages that are accurate and intuitive, you may want to use the advanced technique of automatic writing to get detailed and customized answers.

Automatic writing is the next evolution of journaling. When you write in your journal, you generally write a diary-style account of what is happening in your day-to-day life, as well as your hopes, dreams and fears. If you are consistent, most of the time, you will notice that you start to feel a sense of wisdom about what is going on and you will get insights and solutions to problems while writing. This feeling of wisdom, insight and clarity is your Infinite Self and guides answering you. It comes in the form of journaling, but is actually answered prayer!

Set a Time Each Day

It is so important to journal often and consistently on a daily basis when you are starting out, because your Infinite Self finds a consistent place to communicate with you and through a reliable medium. Personally, I do my writing every morning between 4am and 7am. This is a time when I am wide awake and very clearly receive wonderful and accurate guidance. It is a time where my Infinite Self knows that it has my full attention and there are no distractions.

During my writing sessions, I pour all of my concerns onto the page and then I feel a shift in energy. At that point, I begin to write the answers. This does not come from my "thinking" of solutions. I tune into my Four Clairs and I just write what I feel. Sometimes, it comes as a serious, straightforward message. Sometimes, it is very humorous. But it is always on target and never leads me the wrong way. Once I finish the writing, I go back to sleep and, when I awaken, I look in my notebook to read what I have written. Most of the time, it is a range of between 5 and 30 pages of wonderful insights.

I have been doing this for many years, and it has evolved to so many pages because I am consistent and totally trust what I am getting. You may start out with just a few words, phrases or sentences. But if you persevere and are open, your Infinite Self will definitely come through with amazing answers just for you. It is like you giving your Infinite Self, angels and guides a personal phone number and location to use when there is a message waiting for you. Of course, your intuition is always on and can reach you at any time because it is always sending signals your way.

But the success of automatic writing is based on your attention and receptivity to the message. Journaling regularly invites your Infinite Self to communicate with you consciously. This creates a very powerful and trustworthy relationship.

Now that you are aware of this information, it is really powerful to just *ask specifically* for guidance from your Infinite Self directly in your writing.

The Five Steps to Automatic Writing

1. Set aside a time that you will write each day. It can be for ten minutes or any length of time you want.
2. Get a special notebook that you will use as your journal for your intuitive guidance.
3. Record your questions and concerns with your dominant hand.
4. Close your eyes and take a deep breath. Ask for guidance on what you have written.
5. When you feel ready, take your pen in your opposite hand and begin to write the answers that you get. Just write whatever comes. It may be full sentences or it could also come in the form of a phrase, a word, a color or another symbol.

Using their non-dominant hand is a good way for beginners to be able to discern between their own conscious voice and the voice of their Infinite Self or their angels and guides. If you feel comfortable to write everything with your dominant hand, feel free. Eventually, you will be able to discern exactly when it is your Infinite Self talking instead of your own intellect.

Your Energetic Communication System is so robust and has been put in place to help you access the vast amount of resources that go way beyond our physical realities. When you give it consistent attention you will be able to get more information than you can imagine and you will truly recognize that we are never, ever alone. It is the most powerful set of skills you will ever learn for creating a happy and healthy life!

PART III

CLEARING THE WAY TO GET
ACCURATE MESSAGES

Chapter Thirteen

ENERGETIC HYGIENE TO GET CLEAR GUIDANCE

Accurate intuition depends greatly on how well you are able to identify it from other types of thoughts that come into your mind. Whenever I personally want to make a huge leap forward or get things flowing in a consistent way, I take an inventory in my own life of what needs to be cleared out.

The Dark Side of the Dream

I remember when I wanted to take a major leap in my life, including a big move to a new home, a major career shift and a big positive advancement in my relationship. I sat down and asked myself, "What is the dark side of the dream?" Weird question, right? Usually when we have a big desire, there is also something about that desire that is not so exciting. It could be a fear associated with having that thing or situation come to pass; or it could be something we have to let go of or eliminate to make room for it.

When we are not aware of these often-hidden obstacles, we can start to procrastinate or sabotage our efforts and then misguidedly blame not accomplishing what we desire on something else, such as our worthiness or our capacity to receive what we want. This can be a huge waste of time and often is the cause of people completely giving up on any progression in their lives whatsoever. Once you have come up with your vision of what you desire, your Aha! Factor will turn on to support you in bringing it to fruition.

In many cases the first stop will be to show you what is blocking you and what needs to be cleared out for your dreams to have the space to show up in your world. Your Infinite Self is helping you to accomplish your dreams and goals and also to support you in healing anything that stands in your way, both long- and short-term.

Ask "What Needs to Be Healed?"

One of the best questions to ask right at the beginning of any endeavor is "What needs to be healed in order for me to receive what I am desiring now?" This will give your Infinite Self the freedom to provide you with a clear picture of what needs to be cleaned up as well as to provide you with the tools to do so. When I wanted to make my quantum leap I went into meditation first about my big vision. Then I asked what needed to be healed. I was led to a trio of healers, who each worked with me individually on letting go, self-forgiveness and releasing doubt in my life, to remove the blocks that were standing in the way.

Through this intensive work I discovered some extremely subtle and hidden things, such as a fear of the workload and pressure that success would bring, concern over others who would be jealous or family members who would not be supportive, that had been blocking me energetically and emotionally from fully stepping into what seemed to be a logical plan of action. It was not the glamorous or pretty part of the dream, it was instead the dark side – the underground roots, the foundation of the big bountiful garden that was to come.

I met weekly with my practitioners for sessions and did all of the personal work in between sessions that was prescribed. It was not easy and could be quite frustrating, but session by session I felt lighter. I woke up with amazing insights and my confidence and courage to move forward started to increase dramatically. I found myself easily doing the tasks that I had been procrastinating about for months, and in very short periods of time. I also noticed that my relationships started to get better without any effort at all. As I cleared and shifted my own energy, communication with my loved ones was totally eased up and friends who were just no longer meant to be part of my life moved on without any drama. It was just a natural evolution.

Energy Seeks Its Own Level

Just as water seeks its own level, so does energy. As you get clear from the inside out, your whole outer environment will reflect that. I know it is really tempting to get very attached to our big visions and wish them into existence or work ourselves to the bone to make them happen. But the truth is that if we are willing to get our hands dirty and work to heal our energetic blocks and eliminate clutter, our energy will flow and all that we desire will flow right back to us in seemingly effortless ways.

Clear the Clutter to Boost Your Aha! Factor

On the path to your deepest desires, clearing is always the first step to take in your process of bringing them to fruition. If you get caught up in mentally trying to orchestrate the "how" of it all, you will get stalled and greatly prolong the length of time to accomplish your goals. Clearing your mind and your life of unnecessary clutter is one of the most important steps to take when developing your intuition into a reliable tool and your Aha! Factor into a system of communication you can easily discern and count on. At the beginning, this may feel a bit overwhelming. But as you take each section that we discuss here and clear out the clutter, you will see the benefits almost immediately.

Remember, you do not have to be perfect. You can start off small and then gradually tackle more over time. Each effort to de-clutter will progressively affect the presence and accuracy of your intuition and the accelerated flow of your Aha! Factor.

Clearing the Four Types of Clutter

There are four types of clutter:
  Physical
  Mental
  Emotional
  Energetic

Physical Clutter

A. Your body can hold clutter. Chemicals such as caffeine, sugar, nicotine and alcohol, as well as poor-quality food laden with additives and pesticides, create a great deal of clutter and cause major blocks to receiving the accurate intuition you are looking for. It is important to detox by drinking plenty of pure water and eating organic foods as much as possible, especially fruits, vegetables, meats and dairy products, which are all highly affected by chemicals and additives if not organic. Staying away from artificial sweeteners is also an important step to take when you are clearing your body to better receive accurate guidance and ignite your ability to discern your Aha! Factor.

All of these substances block your energy and slow down your ability to process intuitive information.

B. Physical clutter also affects your space. Your home, work and car environments are the ones where you probably spend the majority of your time. The condition of these three places has a tremendous effect on your ability to get clear and receive accurate guidance from your intuition.

Take an inventory of these spaces. Are they filled with clutter, old items that you no longer use or inefficiently organized? Key places to notice are under beds, in closets and the corners of rooms. When these areas are cluttered, energy gets stuck and it becomes subconscious stress. Overstuffed attics weigh down on you energetically and overstuffed basements create a confused foundation in your life.

I'd now like you to make a list of the areas you feel most need to be cleaned out.

Take care of the worst first

My secret weapon for immediately relieving stress is to tackle the worst first. This will have the greatest effect on freeing up your energy. Once you complete your cleanout, you may want to consult a Feng Shui specialist, who can help you with furniture placement to maximize how your energy flows – they are easy to find online. This is a very powerful way to strengthen your intuition and increase the flow of your Aha! Factor. As your physical environment is cleared, your state of mind relaxes and intuitive information is much easier to detect and understand.

Mental Clutter

Mental clutter is sometimes more difficult to tackle. Mental clutter is the outcome of letting things that you know you need to get done pile up. Taxes, parking tickets, stressful relationships, negative phone calls that focus on problems with friends, leaky faucets (taps) or car repairs that you are procrastinating about can all create mental clutter that gets in the way of having an accurate understanding of your intuition and access to your true guidance.

It is time to make your list and set aside the time to tackle each item. Not only does completion of these types of tasks give you mental freedom, but it also has an even bigger benefit and that is the courage to charge forward unencumbered by the heavy load of uncompleted tasks. When it comes to mental clutter, there are usually a lot of negative judgments that come along with it. Perhaps it is guilt or shame for letting something go that you should have dealt with already. Maybe it is fear of the consequences that gets in your way or anger with yourself for not having finished a mundane task such as paying bills or preparing your tax returns.

These negative feelings and thought patterns are the cause of the clutter and anxiety-rich "mind chatter" that absolutely blocks your capacity to receive the messages that your Infinite Self is sending via your intuition.

Emotional Clutter

Emotional clutter is another area that must be cleared in order to get a more accurate connection with your intuition and increase the flow of your Aha! Factor. Emotional clutter consists of chronic and unmanaged negative states of mind. If you have depression, sadness, unresolved anger, resentment, a tendency to hold grudges or to complain a lot about how everyone else has a problem and you don't, you are dealing with emotional clutter.

Clearing emotions is a bit more challenging than the other areas because, in many cases, we do not realize what we are feeling or the emotions can be so strong that we feel that we cannot control them.

The other challenge is refraining from blaming others for our emotional state of mind. This is perhaps the most disempowering of all. No one is responsible for our happiness. We are ultimately all responsible for how we choose to feel and respond.

Emotional clutter is one of the biggest culprits of misinterpreted intuition. Our intuition is working but our emotions override it and we mistake the emotions for what our intuition is trying to say.

Meditation, yoga and counseling with a reputable energetic healing professional are all good options to consider for emotional clearing. Spiritual psychologists are a new breed of certified psychology professionals who have both the traditional psychology background and credentials, but also incorporate intuition, spirituality and energy work into their practice. This is proving to be one of the most powerful combinations of help for people with a much quicker healing rate than traditional psychology alone.

There are many other types of emotional clearing techniques that are both supervised, such as Theta Healing®, Access Consciousness®, Zero Point Therapy®, hypnotherapy and Emotional Freedom Technique® (EFT), and unsupervised – techniques such as guided meditation CDs and good old-fashioned physical exercise can work wonders.

One of the best ways to clear emotions is to go on a long nature walk in the woods or sit by a large body of water such as the ocean or a lake. This is my favorite way of getting centered and clear when I feel that my emotions are getting the best of me.

Energetic Clutter

The fourth type of obstacle that can stand in the way of your Aha! Factor is energetic clutter. This consists of energetic blocks such as bad karma, the poor energy from others in your environment and your own negative energy. Energetic clutter can be eliminated in a variety of ways.

Most cultures have several processes for clearing spiritual energy. Native Americans used a technique called "smudging." This is a very popular method used by many people throughout the Eastern and Western spiritual communities. In order to smudge, you take good-quality dried sage and burn it in a non-flammable container. The smoke that the sage creates clears the room of heavy and negative energy. (Make sure to open your windows to let all of the negative energy out.)

Some cultures sprinkle salt in the corners of rooms, as well as burn incense such as lavender, rose or Sai Baba Nag Champa – one of the most powerful scents used to balance energy in a room and create a calm and peaceful spiritual environment. Taking a hot sea-salt bath is another way to release toxic spiritual energy. I highly recommend taking hot sea-salt baths to clear your energy and open up your intuitive senses.

Finally, there are many wonderful CDs and downloads to assist in your spiritual clearing. I highly recommend Doreen Virtue's *Karma Releasing and*

Chakra Clearing CDs as well as the writings of Sanaya Roman and Duane Packer, whose books you can find easily online.

My Favorite Detox Bath

Before we move on to the next section I want to share my favorite recipe for a powerful energy-cleansing, hot, salt bath, which is one of the best and super inexpensive ways to give your system a boost. Hot salt baths address all of our systems: they detoxify our physical bodies by drawing out impurities and energetically by clearing our auric fields of blocked energy as well. Additionally sitting in a bath quietly is a wonderful respite for your mind and it gives your emotions a chance to settle down.

I have tried all sorts of combinations and now have an all-time favorite that I am going to share with you.

In the past I have tried pink Himalayan salt, which is great. But this combo is even better because it addresses more things. One of the big additions that I now put in my salt baths is a fresh box of baking soda, which releases any built-up radiation from our bodies. We are constantly exposed to Wi-Fi signals in our homes, cafés, schools and business establishments. And when we use our cell (mobile) phones and microwave ovens or undergo medical procedures, and so on, our bodies are bombarded with energy, which creates a real drag on our systems. The baking soda helps to relieve that drag and release the energy from our systems.

Here is the recipe for you to try. Make up a fresh batch, add your choice of essential oils, fresh flowers or herbs and take a nice 20-minute soak.

You will need:

2 cups (16oz/½ litre) sea salt (do not use iodized salt)
2 cups (16oz/½ litre) Epsom salt
1lb (450g) box of baking soda
Fresh rose petals, lavender or herbs of choice (optional)

If you do not have a tub, you can always make this into a scrub and rub it on your body as you shower. It is not as effective as a bath, but it is definitely better than not doing anything at all.

Be sure to bring a glass of water into the bath with you and sip on it, or drink water with fresh lemon after you finish to replenish your fluids and balance your energy. Water amplifies intuitive information, so don't be surprised if you get a few great Aha! Moments during the bath.

When you get out of the tub, rinse off with a quick shower and use your favorite moisturizer to finish.

Chapter Fourteen

THE AHA! FACTOR
AND YOUR PHYSICAL BODY

Our bodies are complex and they play an integral role in our Energetic Communication System. In addition to providing us with physiological signs in response to our Four Clairs as previously discussed (see pages 99–103), our bodies have very powerful built-in abilities to communicate with us. We can ask telepathically what our bodies require and desire, as well as channel information they would like us to know.

We can also perform certain tests with various substances and our bodies will let us know if they would be beneficial for us or not. Sometimes what doctors, holistic healers, nutritionists and other trusted authorities suggest may make sense on paper, but be completely wrong for our own bodies.

At one point I tried to be a vegetarian because everyone said I should be. I was very strict and miserable with it and gained 40 pounds (18 kilos). When I went to my holistic doctor they suggested that my body needed animal protein. So we performed some muscle testing, an easy to do exercise to see if the protein would be what my body needed or not. The test result strongly stated that being a vegetarian was not for me. And I went back to eating lean animal protein and felt a thousand times better.

Our Bodies Reflect and Support Our Awakening

When we are energetically in tune with our body it makes it much easier to determine what it requires and desires. When we have awakened our Aha! Factor and engaged our Energetic Communication System, that goes even a step further as we are not just consciously focused on our own energetic, mental, emotional and physical needs but are also often perceiving a lot of energy for others as we are more intuitive and empathic. When a major event happens such as 9/11 in 2001, the tsunami in 2004 or Hurricane Sandy in 2012, our bodies go through an enormous amount of turmoil, because not only do we sense what the collective consciousness is going through at the time, but in many cases we also take on the energetic fall-out of the event so that others who can't handle it are relieved.

I know that certain events have particularly hit me hard energetically. I remember in the weeks leading up to Hurricane Irene as the newscasters became more and more emphatic that it was going to be a major storm, I started to get a level of anxiety that does not normally happen. I know my body and what my baseline level of stress is and how high it gets from my normal levels of response. The stress was rising rapidly and I couldn't stop thinking about the storm. I was way more anxious than usual. And I could also feel the energy of the trees and the Earth preparing.

I called all of my colleagues in the energy healing field, the Mystery School and others who I knew could influence energy to say that I thought we should do extra work during that time to deflect the storm, as it felt much more intense than usual. They agreed that they had been feeling the same way and together we all contributed to healing not only the Earth, but also the people who were getting more and more anxious.

As a sensitive, when you are feeling extremely anxious around a world event, it is really important to check in and ask the question "Does this feeling really belong to me, or am I perceiving the anxiety of someone else or the collective energetic grid?" When I started considering that question I realized that what I was feeling really belonged to the masses and to the Earth itself as it prepared for a major shift, not only physically but energetically as well. It was then easier to focus on supporting the people and the planet with a variety of energy work, instead of trying to sort it out as if it was my own. (You can read more details on this in the free report titled "Earth Changes and Stormy Weather," available on the home page of www.TheAhaWay.com.)

As you assimilate all of this energy, your body may go through rapid and sudden shifts of craving for certain foods. If you have been a major meat-eater, you may suddenly desire a vegetarian diet. Passionate vegetarians may all of a sudden start wanting meat with a vengeance. This is a time when you should heed your body's calling as it is seeking balance and fortification in a variety of ways. You may also start craving sugar, salt or more fat content in your foods. Understand that if you ingest these when you are feeling these strong cravings, they will affect your body very positively.

Ask Your Body and It Will Answer

I have a favorite dish called Chicken Bellagio. It consists of breaded chicken cutlets with prosciutto and sautéed arugula (rocket) over a bed of pesto and cream linguine. I eat it about once every nine months or so – not often because for the most part my body does best on a gluten-free diet with absolutely no pasta. I have noticed that if I am in a bad mood or emotionally needy and I eat that dish, my body starts to swell at the table. I feel full and bloated and can't finish it. It clearly has a toxic effect on my body.

But there are some days when I see it on the menu and my body says yes. Then I eat it and I feel light, not full, with no swelling, no extra thirst from the salt and no ill effects, such as night sweats from the gluten. This is simply because it is what my body requires and desires at that time.

My friend Dain and I taught a class called Body Whispering. Dr. Dain Heer, author of one of my favorite books, *Being You, Changing the World*, happens to be an expert at this and teaches that you should always ask your body what it requires and honor that. He says that when you open the menu, the first thing that your eyes focus in on is what your body truly desires. If you honor that, it will taste wonderful. If you don't, whatever you choose will taste horrible and you will have cravings for other things.

So ask your body! That is the way to truly live from the inside out. And as you do this, one of the great side benefits is that, if you are consistent, your body will regulate its own weight.

Water Boosts Your Intuition and Your Ability to Manifest

Water is another substance that your body requires in great quantities. We know that we should have at least eight glasses of water a day for proper hydration. However, it is important, too, to be well hydrated in order to have strong intuition and to receive clear messages from spirit. If you have been feeling blocked, suffering from brain fog or unable to focus, drinking water can help a lot. Also, if you are working on manifesting something big in your life, water is a great amplifier, as it is able to assist you in turning up the volume on your intuition.

Movement

Exercise is a word you may want to remove from your vocabulary. Instead, you may be better off with replacing it with the word "movement." Forcing your body to do exercise that you do not love is not going to do much good. In fact, you may feel sore and tired and have a hard time recovering from your session because it is out of alignment with what your body truly desires.

The best plan is to ask your body, "What type of movement do you desire today?" You may be surprised to hear what it has to say. There will be some days when a gentle walk is what it wants and others a hard-core weight-training session with lots of sweat. If you honor your body when it is asking for a more intense session, you will be surprised at the burst of energy you have, how quickly you recover aerobically and the minimal amount of soreness you will feel the next day.

On the other hand, if you force yourself to stick to a routine conjured up from your logical mind, you may feel heavy, exhausted and quite sore. It is very beneficial to our physical and emotional balance to be flexible, nimble and willing to go with the flow of what our bodies desire and require.

Sleep

Ah, sleep. This is one of the toughest areas for many people, as our sleep patterns can be very unpredictable in our modern-day world with the hyper schedules that we often have. If you are an entrepreneur and can make your own timetable, it makes it a bit easier to honor the sleep patterns your body requires.

Traditionally, according to Western medicine, we should have eight hours of uninterrupted sleep a night to be healthy. And most people get very aggravated if they are not able to sleep for that long. However, sensitives rarely even come close to that.

First of all, our bodies are running on several cycles, as we navigate many dimensions simultaneously. The truth is that while the body shuts down its consciousness for several hours, we don't sleep but shift to being awake in our subconscious and working with our guides in multiple dimensions and parallel worlds where we gather information and bring it back to our physical world.

When we master staying "conscious" during our sleep time, we experience lucid dreaming, astral travel and sometimes out-of-body experiences. We can also use this skill to program our dreams to get information and answers that we seek.

So with all of this potentially going on, can you see why the sleep patterns of a sensitive can be completely different than what is prescribed?

As we become more conscious and interact more actively with our Infinite Selves, we are generally awakened at the same point every morning until we start to pay attention. For many that is a repetitive number like 4:44am, 5:55am and so on. This is a time where people report that they are wide awake and cannot go back to sleep, no matter what they try. It is often misdiagnosed as a stubborn bout of insomnia, which causes more stress because they anticipate being tired all day from the disruption.

As time evolved, especially back in the year of 2012 when we were moving closer to December 21 2012, the historical date where the energetic grid was upgraded and our ability to advance spiritually rapidly accelerated, most sensitives were being awakened two or three times a night in a similar hyper-alert state. This was even more distressful to those who were not aware of what to do. What was happening was not insomnia but a new type of inter-dimensional communication between our embodied self and our Infinite Self via our Energetic Communication System.

For centuries spiritual leaders have known that the veil to intuitive information is thinnest between the hours of 4am and 7am in whatever time zone you are in. As we have evolved physically and energetically the access to this information has vastly increased. So now sensitives who have awakened to their Energetic Communication System are being contacted two or three times a night to provide them with greater volumes of information than ever before.

The best thing to do when you are awakened is to have a journal handy. Write in the journal to get the communication going. As you engage your Energetic Communication System, you may perceive that there is a certain book you should open, a guided meditation you should listen to or some other task such as doing a traditional sitting meditation, yoga and so on. This is the time when your library of spiritual books and recordings will come in handy as your guides can direct you to very specific information that can support you on your way.

I engage in this practice every single day. Sometimes I sleep through as my guides give me time off. But 99 percent of the time I am up and heeding the call. The gift is that as soon as I have completed receiving the message I go back into a very deep sleep and wake up feeling rested and much more fulfilled. Later, I also have the treat of reading the pages that I channeled to see what was said during my sessions and to take in the insights when I am fully awake. That is quite profound.

It can be helpful to think of sleep as a time for inter-dimensional exchange. When we do, our bodies and our minds will feel much more in sync with each other and the day will flow much easier for us. It will also sync up the various aspects of our intuition during our waking day and we will perceive a lot more with much greater ease because we are much stronger through our ability to consciously access our Infinite Self and all of the wisdom it holds.

Having access to your Infinite Self both when you are awake and asleep reduces anxiety and stress, and gives you a much higher rate of actualizing what you most desire, more often and much more quickly than people who only use their logical minds.

Getting regular bodywork is another major requirement for us to live happily and healthily in our modern-day world. Our bodies absorb not only our own stress but also that of others and the Earth. Bodywork, such as massage, saunas, steam baths, hot sea-salt baths and other types of hands-on healing, is extremely helpful to relieving your physical body of toxins and stuck energy.

Similarly, getting energy work, such as reiki healing, cord cutting and many other healing processes, done on your body regularly, helps you to energetically clear and cleanse the residue of the day as well as other people's attachments to your energy. Others can attach to your energy by assigning their happiness to your behavior. You often see this with parental and spousal relationships. Someone will say that they need you to behave a certain way in order for them to be happy or they will try to force you to make a certain choice in order to be happy. Then they focus on you changing your behavior. This creates an energetic attachment that can be very debilitating if not addressed with energy healing.

As sensitives who are in tune with our Aha! Factor, we are often very different from our family members, who in turn put us down or try to force us to be the way they want. We are also very susceptible to the energy of our clients if we take it on as our own. If you are doing readings, bodywork or other types of healing, people can have a tendency to be dead weight on your energy. They come to you with the expectation that you will feed them all the answers and healing they seek without having to carry their own weight. This point of view can be very disempowering to the client and exhausting to the practitioner.

It is really important, even if you are not in the healing or psychic profession, to have a very consistent energetic hygiene routine of regular energy work and clearings to assist you. I go often for a variety of different types of clearing and energy work from reputable professional healers. I also clear the energy of my home with smudging and Epsom salt and alcohol clearings. For my body I take hot sea-salt baths with my special recipe or Himalayan salt and essential oils. In addition, I use aura spritzes daily to infuse my energy with various energetic properties. You can get more information on these at www.TheAhaWay.com.

The Art of Detox

There are times when we need a full-blown detox. This often happens when you are surrounded with people or submerged into situations that are really out of alignment or particularly predatory on your energy. A full detox is when you take time out to clear yourself physically, emotionally, mentally and energetically.

Sometimes I feel overloaded with the news, world events, toxic friends, family or clients or people in general. I start to feel tired, irritable and pessimistic. I often mistake psychic attacks from others as depression or personal sadness, but when I take a closer look and ask the question, "Who does this belong to?" I get the awareness to do a full detox.

For me a full detox consists of eating nourishing foods that my body desires, and does not necessarily involve raw foods, juicing or anything like that, but I pay particular attention to what my body wants, which is often extra minerals, water, a little sugar or salt and extra rest. I add in movement – usually dance or walking in nature, especially by the water or in the rain (weather permitting). I also turn off the phone, the TV and the social media for the day to give myself a chance to reconnect with my own inner voice and find balance.

Affirmation Saturation

One other great thing that works well is to do a modified version of what my friend Sandra Anne Taylor, author of the bestselling book *Quantum Success*, called "affirmation saturation." This is when you say multiple affirmations several times a day to saturate your mind with positive thoughts, so that it naturally switches over to repeating positive things instead of negative loops.

I also put on my iPod and play positive guided meditations, inspiring audio books by various authors and spiritual leaders or go on YouTube and watch inspirational and motivational videos to reconnect with people who are already doing what I like to do with great success. I am non-denominational with my choices: sometimes I need a jolt of Joel Osteen, who focuses on Christian scripture; at other times I look to Rabbi Neruda Berg who focuses on the Kabbalah or to Lee Carroll, who channels Kryon; or I turn to Anthony Robbins who has powerful systems for change; and there are a myriad of others. I have hundreds of audios, videos and books in my toolkit to select from.

I highly recommend that you create your own collection of powerful and inspirational materials for yourself. This is so helpful when you hit that inevitable "wall of stress" that we all encounter at times. The object of the game is not to completely eliminate stress, as that would be impossible in our world, but

175

instead to create systems for ourselves that re-establish and fortify our connections to our Infinite Selves and amplify the communication with our Aha! Factor.

Achieving a Fluid State of Balance

With all of these tools and practices, what we are aiming to achieve is a fluid state of balance. This means that we are not expecting to be or feel the same all of the time or to require the same routines, people and situations to react and relate to us in completely predictable ways. What we are seeking is to be in tune with our energy and higher consciousness using the highest level of intuitive fluency possible, so that we can easily interpret what is ours, what is not ours and what we require and desire on a minute-by-minute basis, so that we can adjust ourselves accordingly as we go.

This fluid state of balance therefore engages a high level of "conscious spontaneity" where we are energetically nimble and able to change direction at a moment's notice, as we feel guided to do so. This is where we can begin to shine and access the very highest and greatest versions of what we most desire with the most ease.

When we have a hard and fast plan that we create only from our minds, without much attention to our greater consciousness, we hit hard walls of resistance and frustration. This then leads to discouragement, depression and giving up on our desires. And when we are out of balance, our bodies are usually the first ones to let us know. We feel anxious, tired, sore, achy, sick, gain or lose weight and can develop many other maladies to let us know that we are off track. Then we start to try all kinds of medications and other interventions that may work temporarily or not at all.

Heal Your Energy and the Rest Will Follow

The best way to begin to heal *any* disruption in your health, wellbeing, relationships, money issues or other things that are off balance is to *ask* for the *healing* of the energy that is causing the symptoms first. Asking for the healing of the energy, whether you are consciously aware of what it is or not, is the most powerful shortcut to complete and reliable change that there is. It is like weeding the garden. When you see dandelions and weeds growing, they will continue to spread if you only pull off the tops. But if you pull them up from the root, they will not grow back. Your healing works the same way. Treating the symptoms with all of the therapy and modalities will not create permanent results. But healing the energy from the core will.

The best way to heal your energy is to set an intention for your Energetic Communication System to provide you with guidance on the very best and most appropriate solutions that are customized specifically for you. And then allow yourself to follow the insights that you get about actions to take.

This is a very simple yet profound approach and it works!

Chapter Fifteen

POTENTIAL BUMPS
ON YOUR PATH

Now that you have a much better idea of what you are capable of when you engage your Aha! Factor, it's time to look at what potential challenges you may have as you learn to navigate and trust your Energetic Communication System. When you are aware of them it will be much easier to handle and you will be able to move forward and not panic if something seems to get in the way.

There are two major categories of potential obstacles. The first are the external obstacles that you may face with other people and outside circumstances. The second are the internal obstacles that arise in your own mind.

The External Obstacles: Naysayers, Skeptics and Dream-killers

Your departure from society's version of normalcy can produce a great deal of anxiety for family and parents, in particular. Many times we are our parents' biggest hope and they use our success and climbing of the career ladder as the validation of how good their parenting was. We are their proof for a job well done. The parents of many sensitives, entrepreneurs, artists and other "out-of-the-norm" types have proclaimed "Oh goodness, where did I go wrong?" while holding the back of one hand on their head and the other holding the heart area. (My mother throws her head back for extra emphasis of the level of despair I have created, and then follows on by 'taking to her bed' in the hope that a long nap will make it go away. Chocolate is also a necessary medication when Mariana is on a roll again.)

Whenever I came to my mom with one of my new ideas, she would sing in her high-pitched voice mixed with cackle, "Off we go into the wild blue yonder!" I would laugh, but also feel an underlying sense of doom for my desires, dreams and ideas because I valued her opinion so much and knew that in my own way I was failing her. Have you ever felt like you were failing your loved ones while living your dreams?

This is often a big part of the sensitive's path. I have had many clients ask me in readings and private coaching sessions, "Mari, how can I get my family to come around? How can I get them to see that what I am doing is great and accept me for who I am?" This is always laced with conflict, anger and anguish.

And usually because of our internal conflict, we are not yet successful enough to prove them wrong, but too far along in loving what we are doing to turn back.

In addition to parents, we have others who may have similar reactions: siblings, bosses, colleagues and friends. So what to do about it?

Build Your Confidence with People of Like Mind

First of all, create a new support system of friends who are successful at doing what you want to do or learn, and those who are seeking the same things as you. Build your confidence in that arena and save any discussions with your friends and family for last, when you are strong, successful and no longer in need of their approval.

Free Will Goes Both Ways

Your independence may threaten loved ones yet illuminate the right path for you. Free will goes both ways. While you have the free will to desire and blaze your trail, they have the free will to dislike what you are doing and to vocalize this. So to go on a crusade to convince them and hold your happiness and self-love hostage until they agree is, at best, crippling.

In order for you to progress you need to let go of the need for others' approval and validation in order to be happy. In many cases we use the lack of others' approval as an excuse to not move forward.

Hidden Self-sabotage

Potential disapproval of family and friends is a great excuse to stay stuck and not make progress on our path into the unknown when our own fears and anxiety flair up. These are distractions that can feel very valid. I know that one of my destructive patterns was always to tell someone who was a naysayer, dream-killer or skeptic about my latest insight, idea or success. I would enthusiastically call them and explain what had happened with joy and they would reply, "Oh that's weird," or "That was a long story, why couldn't you give me the condensed version?" or some other dismissive response. That child-like wonder in me would then be crushed and I would often shelve the project or start to doubt myself.

Then, I would go for a walk in nature, go to the bookstore and read something inspirational or watch motivational videos of people who were successful and talk with someone who "got it" to get back on track. One thing I can say is that my passion and my guides always were pulling me forward. And eventually I realized that I was using this cycle as a way to sabotage what I was doing and stay behind with the people I loved. I didn't want to be different from everybody because I thought I would be lonely.

But one day that all changed. I remember attending one of the Abraham Workshops channeled by the very popular and talented channel, Esther Hicks. She was addressing this conflict of not wanting to change too much for fear of being lonely. And she said, "It is very lonely on the leading edge of thought." So do not expect much support from all of your loved ones as you go along.

One other thing I have found is that the complexity of the lives of many sensitives stepping onto the path is greatly reduced. After the initial departure from the "ladder of success," we often let go of all sorts of things that tie us down and clutter us up. I sold my home and reduced expenses so I did not have to keep a corporate job, which was absolutely killing me. I gained a great deal of weight the year after my fiancé died and was miserable staying in that terrible environment. I moved three times so that I could find a space that was nurturing to me as I lived the life of a budding sensitive and entrepreneur. I knew that working for someone else was not for me. That does not mean that there are not plenty of sensitives who are happy to work for others and thrive, it was just not the best option for me and I went on to develop my businesses. It was not for the faint of heart and involved a lot of sacrifice from myself and my family, who supported me in lean times. But it was for me a matter of life and energetic death. I had to stay nimble and follow my path.

Let Things Take Their Course

What is most important is to not jump to hasty conclusions. You do not have to immediately quit your day job to go open a yoga studio. There is a legitimate time of exploration and discovery that needs to take place and this can be done at your own pace. You will know when it is time to move forward in new directions. And choosing to follow this path does not mean that you have to change jobs at all.

The question to ask yourself is "Does this make my heart sing?" If the answer is yes, then stay; if it is no, then it is time to create a plan, engage your Aha! Factor and follow its guidance on how to go forward. And setting an intention to have your next steps revealed to you and being willing to follow them is all that you need to get started.

Don't Ignore the Messages

There are two voices going on inside your head, the voice of your Infinite Self and the voice of your logical mind. The logical mind holds the voice of the inner critic, the opponent that always wants to play it safe, keep you stuck and stunt your growth and forward mobility.

The critic is very clever and can mask and disguise itself in so many ways. It says things such as: "Are you nuts? You can't do that. It's not logical," "You better not try that; it never works," "That's too good to be true," and thousands of other things that undermine your confidence. The critic keeps itself alive in your head by feeding off negative emotions like fear, confusion, panic, over-analysis, anger and depression. It encourages procrastination, criticism and just plain giving up and settling for the status quo.

Your Aha! Factor is the enemy of the critic. Your Energetic Communication System carries the voice of your Infinite Self. It is the accurate language you use to communicate with the part of yourself that is in the physical body and under its constraints. Your Aha! Factor is always right because it comes from your Infinite Self, which has access to all things and all information. It is efficient. It provides you with a strong feeling, a knowing and a sense of empowerment. Your Aha! Factor may not give you the answer you most want to hear, but it will give you the right answer for your highest and greatest good.

It does not do your Infinite Self any good to have you confused and searching forever! That greater part of you will always give you the most efficient and accurate answer first. It may lead you down what seems like a side path from what you thought you wanted, but the new path usually holds necessary information or lessons that you need to learn in order to reach your ultimate goal. You will see that it turns out to provide you with what I like to call a "cosmic shortcut" if you just trust and take action.

Acting Leads You to Answered Prayer

When we pray, do yoga or tai chi, meditate, say affirmations, perform rituals and ask for spiritual assistance from various other practices, we hope for results in the form of *answered prayer*.

Typically, we have many questions:

1. When will our answers come?
2. How will it all end up?
3. Will the issue be miraculously solved all at once?
4. Was that incident or encounter a sign of progress or just a coincidence?
5. What are the pros and cons?
6. What are the options?
7. Which is the best way to go?

It is time to trust in your Divine guidance and take inspired action instead of over-thinking and intellectualizing your concerns.

Inspired Action

Have you ever noticed that when you are trying to sort out a big problem and you finally give up, you get this big insight about what to do and somehow just "know" that this is the right way to go? So you take the next step with a keen sense of faith and trust, without any real idea how it will end up but feeling it is simply the right thing to do at the time? This is *inspired action* coming from your Infinite Self.

Fear and Control-based Action

However, sometimes you lose your way. You feel anxious, confused, overwhelmed. You try to use your logic and disengage your feelings to make a "good, rational decision based in reality." You start to try *this* out or *that* out; you ask for advice from friends, family or experts. You collect opinions but, try as you may, you still can't decide what to do. Or what you choose based on this process seems to lead you to a dead end. Your inner critic creates this intellectualized action based on the fear of making a mistake.

The Critic versus Your Infinite Self

Your inner critical voice undermines your intuition and short-circuits your ability to perceive your Aha! Factor. The original purpose of the critic was to protect you from harm and danger. It was meant to help you to be discerning and give you the ability to protect yourself. However, discernment is different than criticism.

Being prudent and considering the emotional, physical and energetic safety of a situation comes from the guidance of your Infinite Self, not the inner critic.

This energy of discernment is easy to recognize because it comes from a position of stability and strength. You feel powerful and have a sense of personal empowerment when you are doing your due diligence about a given situation.

However, the critic represents the opposite of your Infinite Self, because it is the part of us that wants to keep things the same and stop you from progressing any further. In the beginning, when you are just discovering your intuition, your critic will disguise itself as a variety of things.

The Top 21 Ways Your Critic Masks Itself

It is important to note that our Aha! Factor and Energetic Communication System are always on. They never turn off, regardless of what we do. However, our ability to recognize and perceive what they are communicating can be greatly affected by our negative thoughts and emotions.

The following list provides you with 21 of the most notorious causes of blocked intuition.

1 **Fear** Sometimes what we are feeling is not fear but excitement for a new shift or change. However, fear can also be real and can mask itself in many different ways.

2 **Self-doubt** One of the biggest causes of not being able to discern what is our true intuition is doubting our ability to receive correct information.

3 **Second-guessing** This is similar to self-doubt because we get a clear message from our inner guidance and all of the signs to go with it, but keep asking as we don't yet have complete proof that it is going to turn out the way we expect.

4 **Guilt** When we feel like we don't deserve good things or feel unworthy in general, we can easily block our ability to discern what our intuition is communicating.

5 **Competition** Being competitive with others sends a signal that we feel there is not enough to

go around. This type of thinking stems from our inner critic and is not coming from our intuitive energy at all.

6 **Condemnation of others** Condemning others is also coming from our ego and has us swimming in negative emotions and thoughts. This quickly shuts down our ability to perceive our intuition.

7 **Self-righteousness** One big trap to our forward progression and intuitive sensitivity is to feel that *our* way is the *only* way to think or be. Taking a stance that everyone should believe in what we believe in is a sure way to set up blocks to receiving in our own lives. People should be allowed to believe in what resonates with them. Their choices may be different than ours and that does not weaken the truth of what we believe. Live and let live.

8 **Self-aggrandizing** There is a big difference between self-confidence and self-aggrandizing. When we put ourselves on a pedestal, we not only alienate ourselves physically but we also shut down our ability to receive energetic information as well. The more confidence we have, the less we need to talk about it.

9 **Gossip** This can be extremely damaging to our energy and our ability to receive accurate information from our intuition. When we spend time talking about others, especially with negative emotion and intention, we are shutting down our receptivity and our ability to hear our own inner voice.

10 **Unexpressed anger** Anger can be very appropriate at times, especially when it is expressed constructively. However, when it goes unexpressed we can often turn it on ourselves and set up a big obstacle to being able to hear the Divine guidance that is waiting for us at all times.

11 **Depression** This, together with grief, blocks our receptive centers and puts us in an often all-consuming space of self-sabotage and unworthiness. When this type of negative spiral occurs it can be very easy to mistakenly believe that our Aha! Factor has shut down and our intuition does not exist.

12 **Chaos and confusion** I had a friend who absolutely thrived on chaos and confusion in her life. She always had massive issues going on in every category – finances, relationships, career, parenting and health issues were always swirling. The stress she was under was

unfathomable to most people. Yet she thrived in this negative vortex of energy. Whenever things started to stabilize in one area, she would find drama in another. What I realized was that she truly did not want to know what her intuitive voice was saying. Instead, she wished to stay disconnected and in a state of complete chaos. This enabled her to blame everything on circumstances and not take responsibility for creating her own situation. This is one of the most damaging ways to block your intuition. The best place to get accurate support from your Aha! Factor is in silence.

13 **Procrastination** This is a big drain on energy and is usually a sign of fear or apprehension. The main reason why procrastination can be detrimental to us is that we start to feel guilty, worried, ashamed, pressured or any number of other negative emotions, and this gets in the way of our ability to discern what our intuitive energy is trying to communicate. However, we will often get signs to move forward that are not particularly pleasant if we are procrastinating about something that will help us to move forward. Our Infinite Self will continue to communicate with us to get us to go in the right direction.

14 **Unworthiness** Feeling that we do not deserve to move forward or that we somehow have to be "special" in order to receive guidance can shut down our capacity to discern the communication.

15 **Rushing** A sense of urgency to get something done can be great. However, rushing through to try and force an outcome or pushing to make something happen shuts down our receptivity and ability to tell if what we are connecting with is anxiety or intuitive guidance.

16 **Over-committing** When we over-extend ourselves and fill up our schedule with too many extraneous tasks, we block our energy flow. We can also have a tendency to take on other people's issues and lose our energetic boundaries, which is a sure way to get confused about what our intuition is trying to say.

17 **Obsession** This is when we try to control an outcome and allow it to take over our thoughts, to the point where it is completely disruptive to everything else. When we obsess, we truly arrest our forward progression until we get what we are focusing on. This is very damaging to our ability to receive any guidance energetically.

18 **Addiction** When we are addicted to anything, be it food, alcohol, drugs, cigarettes and so on, we are turning to something outside of ourselves for relief and numbing our senses. This causes us to completely shut down to receiving our true guidance.

19 **Excessive worry** This is negative prayer. When we go over and over the same thoughts with a sense of anxiety and heavy emotions we are spinning the energy in the wrong direction and can put up unnecessary barriers that make it very difficult for our intuition to break through.

20 **Victim mentality** Feeling that we are a victim of circumstance and not being willing to take any responsibility for what we are creating in our world can be a real drain and barrier to having a consistent flow of our Aha! Factor. Our communication with our Infinite Selves relies on feeling a sense of personal power and trust in the wisdom that is available to use beyond our physical world.

21 **Catastrophizing** When things seem to be taking a tough turn, we can be tempted to think about all of the worst-case-scenario outcomes. This is called catastrophic thinking and can immobilize us from moving forward. The fear and anxiety can be completely overwhelming and this is

the time when we need to be in touch with our intuition the most. Getting out in nature, drinking water and taking some quiet time will enable us to tune in to that intuitive voice and get a much more realistic perspective on what is going on.

There are several characteristics that you should be aware of so that you can tell if your critic is masking itself to sound like a wise intuitive voice or if your intuition is speaking to you.

The Top 10 Ways to Recognize Your Critic

1   The critic is loud and sporadic.

2   The critic speaks using lots of words and analysis.

3   The critic creates feelings of fear, anxiety and worry.

4   The critic causes you to second-guess yourself.

5   The critic speaks with the words "should" or "should have," and refers to the past or what could happen in the future.

6   The critic attempts to make you competitive, or to feel shame or guilt.

7   The critic comes in gradually, starting off as worry and then growing to full-blown anxiety attacks.

8   The critic drains your enthusiasm and energy.

9   The critic seems off-base and out of context.

10   The critic feels very disempowering.

The Top 10 Ways to Spot Communication from Your Aha! Factor and Your Infinite Self

1   Your Aha! Factor is the consistent and usually quiet voice within you that often repeats itself.

2   Your Aha! Factor speaks using symbols, feelings, senses and signs.

3   Your Aha! Factor creates a sense of validation, knowing and overall peace, even if the message is not necessarily one that you want to hear.

4   Your Aha! Factor creates a sense of knowing and inspiration.

5   Your Aha! Factor focuses on the present moment.

6   Your Aha! Factor wants you to feel proud and complete, knowing that there is abundance for everyone.

7   Your Aha! Factor feels like a sudden Aha! Moment in response to a prayer or an affirmation.

8   Your Aha! Factor infuses you with high energy and the immediate desire to move forward.

9   Your Aha! Factor feels familiar and comforting.

10 Your Aha! Factor feels empowered and resolved.

Working on strengthening your intuition will help you to distinguish the difference between the voice of your Infinite Self and the voice of the inner critic. This is easier than it seems. Make the time to regularly attend to your energetic hygiene (see pages 154–162) and master the recognition of your energetic senses, the four clairs (see pages 99–103).

It also helps to take the time each day to get quiet and listen. Your Infinite Self is always communicating with you and guiding you via the language of your intuition, but it is really helpful when you slow down the chatter of your mind and critic, as this gives you the space to connect with your Aha! Factor. Then your Aha! Factor can flow throughout the day and you will become much more aware of it as this happens.

Chapter Sixteen

BUILDING TRUST
AND CONSISTENCY

Now that you are clear about what you would like to accomplish and how your Energetic Communication System operates, it is time to put all that you have learned into daily practice. While there may seem to be a lot of details to remember, it can help to organize the most important daily practices that you need to do in order to benefit from the guidance of your Aha! Factor.

Be Clear on Setting Your Intention or Asking Questions

All it takes to get things moving is to state an intention or to ask a question. Once you do so, you give your Energetic Communication System permission to gather your guidance and provide you with the inspired actions that you should take to achieve success.

Since all of your repetitive thoughts that are accompanied with strong emotion can potentially register on the energetic grid as an intention, it is really important to be clear on what you are asking. You will have several intentions and questions going at the same time as well. Some will be for the small, mundane things such as finding your keys or deciding what to eat for an energy-enhancing breakfast. Others will be about the big stuff like finding the right job to make your heart sing, or a new romantic partner.

Everything counts when you are working with energy. So be sure to keep that in mind and edit as many of your negative thoughts as possible by shifting your focus to something positive.

Using Your Aha! Factor for Creative Problem-solving

This is where your new skills will really start to come in handy. If you have a problem or a challenge that you are finding difficult to sort out, try asking one or more of the following questions or making one or more of the following statements:

1. What do I need to know most right now for a quick solution?
2. What can I do now to accelerate getting a solution?
3. Do I need to take any action at this time?

4. Do I just need to wait and see at this time?
5. Please bring me the information that I need to know right now to reach a quick resolution.
6. Please show me signs, symbols and synchronicities so that I know beyond a shadow of a doubt which direction I should take or what the truth of the situation is.

How to Get Help with Stubborn Situations

When working with your ECS, remember that there are many layers of activity going on simultaneously. Often things need to be configured and events, resources and people lined up in Divine order according to Divine timing, so that you not only get what you need, but also learn the lessons you are to garner from the situation. Sometimes the only answer is to have patience and wait for the signs that things are shifting.

Here are some of the questions to ask and a statement to make when you are faced with seemingly stubborn situations.

1. What is the truth of this situation? Or, please give me clarity on the situation at hand and what I should do next. (Be sure that you really want to know the truth before you ask. Sometimes you

do not get an answer because subconsciously you do not want to know!)

2. Am I missing information on how to do something?
3. Is there a mental, physical, emotional or energetic block that needs to be cleared?
4. What is the next set of steps that I need to take?
5. State: I am open to receive and willing to accept all of the guidance that my Energetic Communication System has for me now.

When sorting out stubborn problems, writing in your journal and exercising outside in nature are particularly helpful. And when writing in your journal you can express your anxiety, frustration and so on about the issue, which releases it from your energy, creating space for the solution. The movement in exercising creates a flow of energy and you also breathe more deeply as you move, especially outdoors. The next step is to let the problem go and distract yourself with something else. This keeps you from getting in the way of the solution flowing to you as quickly as possible.

For the Big Dreams

Now that we have covered the day-to-day basics, let's discuss tackling how to break down those dreams into smaller pieces to reach your long-range goals.

Take the results from your Perfect Day Exercise we did in Part I of the book (see p. 84).

What is your number one priority? Let's say it is to buy a new home.

First, you want to get focused on what type of home you desire, where you would like it to be and, most importantly, how you would like to feel when you are in it. Then you can simply say, "I employ my Energetic Communication System to show me the steps I need to take to bring this to fruition." Each day you can take some time to envision what it feels like to already be living in the home of your dreams. And your intuition will start to send you signals of what to do to move things forward.

When you are working toward your bigger goals that may take a bit longer to configure, be aware that it is very easy to fall into the trap of trying to figure out how to do it. It can get very discouraging if you let your logical mind take over and overshadow the subtle signs that your Aha! Factor presents. So be sure to give yourself the quiet time to receive the true guidance from your ECS. It will come in the form of your intuitive senses and signs, symbols and synchronicities will point the way to the inspired-action steps you need to take. And you will know, too, by the physiological feelings you get in your body: if you get an idea and goose bumps at the same time, you know that is energetically guided and you should take action immediately. If, however, you are feeling tense, stressed out, anxious or panicky and start to feel ideas from that place with no positive energy, pull back and settle down. Take a walk or a hot bath, or some other type of energetic hygiene and wait until you get a genuine directive from your Aha! Factor. Rest assured, it will come.

One other thing to remember is that your Energetic Communication System will often lead you to things in ways that you could never think of yourself. Sometimes you will be led into what seems like a side door or a dead end. But when you look more closely it turns out to be a shortcut. You may be led to meet a particular person or to get a new skill that will help you in the long run and keep you safe.

Be patient and follow the signs. Keep journaling so that you can identify patterns in what is happening, and connect the dots. Your journal is an invaluable tool when working on creating your big dreams, so keep it close at hand.

A Day in the Life of Using Your Aha! Factor

Although there are an infinite number of possibilities, I want to give you a sample of what an average day may look like when you are engaging the Energetic Communication System on a regular basis.

When you wake up in the morning

- As you are waking up, make a note of any memories of dreams that you had in the night, or any song lyrics, new hunches or ideas.
- Journal three pages to get your Aha! Factor moving and to express any concerns that your mind has in writing so they stay out of your way.
- You can also write a bit about what you would like to accomplish in the day and any questions that you have for your guides.

Energetic hygiene

In the morning it is always good to consider doing a short meditation or clearing exercises to make sure you are open to receive what you are asking for. You do not have to tackle everything all at once, but using a bit of sea salt in your morning shower, smudging your body or taking a quick walk outdoors is a great way to keep things clear and get the energy flowing. Do whatever makes you feel light and focused.

Throughout the day

As you move forward through your day, pay close attention to your intuition. You may have a quick flash of insight, a bit of a daydream that gives you a clue, hear song lyrics that make sense to you or experience some sort of synchronistic event that lets you know you are on the right track. Remember that if you see or hear something three times, then it's a sign.

You may also get the idea to look at a particular book or to listen to a certain audio on your iPod that may provide you with inspiration. Heed these types of hunches. They can be great shortcuts for getting vital information to you.

Pay close attention to any hunches that you get to do things differently than you normally do. For example, if you get an urge to take a different route to work, followed by a feeling of lightness, follow the hunch. If you go to order your usual morning coffee at the local coffee shop and all of a sudden feel like trying something different, do so. This is often your body's way of letting you know that it would benefit from a different substance that day. It also will keep you in tune to listening with your energy, not just with your head.

Remember to continue to pay attention to how your body feels and what signs it is providing – it is a very reliable psychic antenna and will always let you know the truth of a situation.

Managing negative thoughts

If you feel that you are getting into a tug of war with your inner critic or with negative people, stop! Take some time – maybe 10 minutes – to be quiet, breathe deeply for several breaths and ask your intuition for clarity. Do not panic, as these thoughts generally pass quickly, especially if you focus on your intention to stay connected to your intuitive guidance instead.

Pay attention to your thoughts to receive telepathic messages

Remember that you are connected to everyone energetically and can communicate with them non-verbally through your telepathic abilities. If you get an intuitive feeling to reach out to someone, you may want to follow it and contact them. It is validating to hear that they, too, were thinking of you.

Practice your automatic writing to get in-depth guidance

You can do this in the morning or at night as you desire and feel drawn to do it. Your ability to tap into the stream of consciousness that provides you with highly customized guidance via channeling gets stronger as you practice consistently. I personally have a specific time each morning when I work with my guides via channeling. They show up very reliably each day and it has developed into a powerful connection that I can tap into at any time for any reason whatsoever. Channeling is a wonderful resource and when you develop this skill you will be able to apply it to all of your creative endeavors as well.

Energetic hygiene at night before going to sleep

Before you go to sleep is a great time to do a quick clearing to cut any emotional cords you have acquired during the day or to intentionally let go of things that do not serve you.

Do not watch anything stressful on the TV at this time, as it causes a drag on your energy. And you want to be as light as possible so that you can potentially receive guidance in your dreams.

Also take some time to express gratitude for the things you are blessed with and let yourself fall asleep with joyful intentions as your predominant thoughts.

Of course, this is just a sample of how you can engage your Aha! Factor throughout the day, so feel free to adapt it all to suit your own needs. The most important thing is to give your energetic systems care and attention, so that you can accelerate receiving what you desire and live with much greater ease!

Joy is not mandatory for having great success

Most people have a false idea of what joy is. They feel that we should be striving to be "joyful" 100 percent of the time. This is not realistic and it is not the real goal. Life is dynamic. We all have highs and lows. So it is not practical to attempt to avoid the lows and stay in a static state of joy.

The true goal is to be able to flow with whatever life brings your way and to stay connected to your guidance through your Energetic Communication System. Staying present, centered and neutral during difficult times is one of the most powerful life skills that you can develop. When you are able to do this, you are able to garner the lessons quickly and succinctly. You collect the wisdom, discard the rest and move on.

The ability to "go with the flow" is true freedom. No one can take that away from you. This state of being is your greatest Divine gift and it is the ultimate goal of your Infinite Self. Mastering the language of your intuition and feeling truly connected to your Infinite Self with consciousness is being able to communicate and manage creatively through the difficult times as well as also fully enjoying the joyous times without doubt and fear. Can you imagine what you can accomplish this way?

Managing the moment

One of the key things to remember is that your Aha! Factor – your true inner voice – can only be found in the "present moment." Your critic can be found only dwelling on the past and speculating on the future. So if you are feeling calm, centered and knowing, it is because you are in the present moment.

If you are feeling confused, worried or frightened, it is probably because you are focused on something that happened in the past or are fearful about something that could happen in the future. Both of these are where the critic resides. And it always tries to draw you out of the present moment where you can find your true strength.

How to quickly get back to the present moment

The most important thing to do is to check in with yourself often. The best way to make sure that you are in the present moment is to take three slow, deep breaths. I always put my hand on my heart, close my eyes and take the three slow, deep breaths. This immediately brings you into the present. It also disengages the critic and engages your awareness of your Aha! Factor.

This tiny little gesture is one of the most powerful habits you can establish in order to create that trustworthy two-way communication with your intuition that you are seeking.

210

PART IV

ENLIGHTENED LIVING WITH YOUR AHA! FACTOR

Chapter Seventeen

THE 7 PILLARS OF ENLIGHTENED LIVING

Over the years I have been on a personal quest to find my way through life and harness the power that I knew innately we all have. I could just never accept that there was only one way to live and, by trial and error, I discovered the tools that I have shared with you.

I have organized all that we have discussed so far into what I now refer to as the 7 Pillars of Enlightened Living. They are:

1 Fluency in Your Energetic
   Communication System
2 Energetic Hygiene
3 Your Aha! Toolkit
4 Contribution
5 Fellowship
6 Sanctuary
7 Love and Relationships

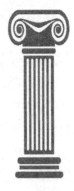

When we put these in place we have the complete foundation to easily create all that we desire. Remember, you do not have to be perfect! Just being aware of these components is a great start and as you develop you will find yourself focusing on one area or another. At this point I flow through all of these very fluidly throughout each day.

Let's go into more detail about what each pillar represents.

1 Fluency in Your Energetic Communication System

As we have discussed, the most important skill to master is becoming fluid in the language of your intuition. This is our connector to our Infinite Self. It is our key to understanding all that is available, what we should move forward on and what to avoid. Energetic fluency also links us into the ongoing conversation that the entire world participates in. As all the world whispers, when you know how to interpret this language you will always know that you are never truly alone. Of course, you will also be able to make decisions and choices that may have really stumped you in the past with much greater ease.

Perhaps the most important benefit is that you are much safer when you have energetic fluency. The Universe has all sorts of ways to protect you, from telling you with a clairaudient voice to stop on a curb to avoid being hit by an oncoming car, to your body letting you know what herb or food it requires to head off a cold. This is invaluable and will save you so much potential pain, time, heartache, money and stress. No matter what you need, you name it and your intuition will help. It applies to absolutely everything!

Sometimes we need to incorporate tools and reputable professionals to assist us in interpreting our intuitive messages. Having a set of my Intuitive Living Oracle Cards or a good set of Angel Oracle cards are great tools to have on hand that can give you a boost of confidence with interpreting what you perceive. We will discuss this further in Pillar 3: Your Aha! Toolkit.

2 Energetic Hygiene

As we have discussed earlier (see pages 151–162), one of the keys to mastering your energetic fluency is to create a consistently clear environment so that you can have the best chance of receiving accurate guidance. This applies to being clear mentally, physically, emotionally and energetically. And it is quite easy to do in most cases. Of course, no one is perfect, as life is a dynamic process of ebbs and flow. So there are times when we are super-organized and other times when we are not.

I can always tell that something needs to be tended to when I start to feel hazy, foggy, sleepy, cranky or just flat-out confused. When I start to feel any of these things I take a quick inventory in my mind and ask, "What needs to be cleared here?" Believe it or not, one stuck situation could require some clearing in all four categories.

For example, if I find that I am feeling overwhelmed, I can often trace back and see that I have some organizing to do in my house, am in need of an emotional cord cutting, need a soothing, hot salt bath for my body, a good clearing of the energy in my house and to write down a to-do list for my logical mind to create a game plan to sort out the details and get things done.

Additionally, there are times that we may need professional help when it comes to clearing in any of these areas. As I mentioned before, it's good to know the difference between going to the dentist for a professional cleaning and brushing your teeth and flossing in between visits.

3 Your Aha! Toolkit

It is really important to create your own personal toolkit of resources, tools, books, recordings, DVDs, practices and reputable practitioners to turn to. When you create this personal library you have something you can turn to 24 hours a day, seven days a week. This is invaluable for creating an enlightened lifestyle.

It's important to remember that life is not a static process. It is very dynamic and constantly changes because there are so many variables that shift minute by minute. And no one person, book or recording has all of the answers. This is one of the reasons why I produce and host radio, TV and Telesummits. I have worked with thousands of clients during readings and private sessions. With this intensive work, I realized that I could only get a person so far on their path because everyone needs a different recipe to support them wherever they are in their own process.

I found that the angels and guides would provide a different prescription for every client. Some would do super well with a particular practitioner or healer, while others would not resonate with them at all. One book would be a fountain of wisdom for one client, yet another could not even get through the first chapter.

While many people seek gurus, magic bullets and one-size-fits-all solutions, you can never achieve enlightened living this way. Why? Because with every single thought, feeling and emotion that we have, we change. We attract different people, situations and circumstances with every breath. And this dynamic state requires that we are nimble, that we have plenty of options and tools to support us for a vast variety of circumstances.

I, personally, love books and have over a thousand titles. But I love audios even more because I have a very busy schedule and it is much easier for me to listen to someone speaking while I do other things than to have to sit down and read. When I find something I really resonate with I will often get both the book and the audio. I have a full iPod and have only actually bought five songs! The rest of the content is audio recordings of my favorite spiritual advisors, personal-development gurus and New Thought leaders, as well as inspirational content. I have many workshops, guided meditations and process loops on my iPod as well. At any point of the day or night, I have resources right at my fingertips to turn to. And this is tremendously helpful.

One of the key causes of procrastination, anxiety and angst is just missing information on how to do something, rather than laziness or a lack of talent or discipline like we are often taught to believe. In most cases you don't need willpower, you need support. And when you have the how-to instructions or can clear the anxiety with a guided meditation, you can connect in with your Energetic Communication System, find your center and accelerate forward so much more quickly.

Another benefit of having your own well-researched and customized toolkit is the sense of personal power it gives you. When you have done your research and you have tested the waters with a variety of reputable people, you are empowered to choose what works for you at that point in time, instead of blindly following just one person and giving them all of your power to make your decisions and choices.

That is why I produce and host shows, because I have done the same thing. And I like to share the best of the best with my audiences so they have access to more tools for themselves. I also think that you do not have to stick with just one type of modality or doctrine. What I have seen is that different practitioners hit the spot for what we need at different times. Some days you may feel uplifted by listening to Doreen Virtue do a guided meditation with the angels, while on another day you may feel totally inspired by a sermon from Joel Osteen. We all have different messages and styles, but we are also all connected. So just as we have a wardrobe that includes clothing that is appropriate for a variety of activities, different types of weather and so on, we can have a whole boutique of options in our library to deal with any circumstance that we encounter.

One last point to make here is that at times we outgrow the resources we have. So what you learned last year from one practitioner or teacher doesn't feel like it is effective the next year. This is perfectly normal as there are many different levels of teachers and types of study. Likewise, there are times when we can come back to something in our library that we haven't touched upon in a long time, re-listen to it and find that it has a whole different meaning or application in our lives now than it did the first time around. This can also be a great way to measure how much progress we have made over time. Always check in with your ECS to see if something is the right fit for you.

4 Contribution

In my own life, for quite some time I concentrated on the first three pillars. Even though I was working in the spirituality field, I was feeling so depleted by my work and so focused on my own development that it was not registering that I was making a contribution. And then something shifted.

One day I was hosting a show and the conversation changed to applying the modality that we were discussing to the Earth and not just to the individuals listening to the show. Normally we have a speaker and people call in and ask questions, which usually center on their own personal circumstances and issues. This can be enriching for some and boring for others who are not at the same stage or circumstance. But such is the nature of a show that offers audience questions and answers.

On this particular show I could feel a completely different energy welling up. The conversation was about a particular energy healing modality, which focused on using light to heal, that the practitioner had channeled and how he was using it to heal people very successfully around the world. This series was targeted at advanced spiritual seekers and the types of questions were of a totally different nature than the usual shows.

Instead of the questions being focused on individual problems, the audience started to ask about how we could apply this particular modality to the Earth, to the oceans, to the animals and more. It was an amazing development. And the show was extraordinarily successful. That was when I finally felt, "Wow! I have the energy to take this work to the next level." When I retraced my steps that led up to this shift I realized that I had personally had several breakthroughs in the weeks and months leading up to the show. And I was feeling less bogged down. It was as if my cup was finally full enough to be able to share without feeling drained and depleted, which had been a chronic problem for me for several years.

When we engage our Aha! Factor, master the first three pillars and integrate them as a part of our daily lives, we create more energetic space. By space I mean we are less stressed, we have more tools to help us when we need them in the ways that are really relevant to what we are going through and we know how to keep our energy clear so we can receive accurate guidance and have a flow of signs, symbols and synchronicities guiding us throughout our day. This relieves stress and opens up reserves of energy that we can then share and contribute to others, both in our personal lives and the world at large.

Contribution comes in many forms. You may be part of delivering an intuitive message for someone else. You may provide philanthropic support or create a business that really comes from your heart and makes a difference in the world. Your contribution may be allowing yourself to create art or music or bring an invention to fruition. It may be to just contribute joyful or peaceful energy to others and let that ripple out onto the energetic grid, creating more positive energy in the group consciousness over all.

This spaciousness for contribution is where your dreams can truly see the light of day, where they can incubate and then come to fruition. This spaciousness also enables you to hear your inner voice that lets you know that you truly matter, that what you are inspired to create is coming from your Infinite Self, which is connected to all things, and that is what we are all here for. This is the true meaning of "your cup runneth over" – when you *have* more energy, you can *contribute* more and that is good for everyone.

5 Fellowship

This pillar presented itself to me in meditation and it was something that I had been taking for granted. Most of the time when we hear the word "fellowship" we think of a traditional church. This word applies to the congregation and how they contribute to and support each other and the mission of the church.

What I find is that when people choose to walk away from organized religious organizations and follow a "spiritual path" they are often running from the rules, judgments and doctrines that went along with being a part of that group. And when they start to explore new options, they often avoid communing with a group of people because it feels "too organized."

Over the years my path became very lonely. I started in the mid-1980s and was a pioneer in many ways, especially among my peers, who were getting married, having families and climbing traditional career ladders. I found myself either not speaking about what I was doing, being ridiculed by family members or probed for answers by friends who wanted to tap into my intuitive abilities to solve their own problems. This was a very challenging time that lasted for years, until I learned how to do two things. One was to set boundaries, so I was not being used for free readings and constant advice that went unreciprocated. And the second was to create a community of like-minded individuals with whom I could have fellowship.

At first the community started out with me as the leader and a handful of wonderful clients who were of a like mind. Over the years, The Aha! Moments Global Community has become an international fellowship of tens of thousands of members from 95 countries around the world, as well as close to 150 amazing colleagues, who are authors, speakers, New Thought and inspirational leaders, healers and energy practitioners.

I have found that the leaders who have the most success, not only professionally but personally, have found fellowship to be an integral part of their world. So even though you may have been avoiding getting connected to a group, it can be a very healthy and wonderful addition to your personal development, joy and wellbeing. You just need to choose carefully and always maintain your ability to think independently by developing the other four pillars that we have outlined here.

When you are fluent in your intuition and have that diverse spiritual toolkit, you will not get sucked into the wrong group or taken in by self-serving leaders who are more into control or being a guru for their own gain. Your intuition will also let you know when you have outgrown a group or a situation and it is time to move on to a new one that is more appropriate.

6 Sanctuary

I just love the process of writing in communion with your Infinite Self, angels and guides. As I was finishing the previous pillar they brought another one to my attention – and that is sanctuary.

The environment that we create to operate in on a daily basis is our sanctuary. And this is extremely important to our wellbeing and in order to receive clear guidance from our Energetic Communication System.

When we first think of sanctuary what often comes to mind is a beautiful home with a meditation room and elegant furnishings, as well as plants, gardens, pools and fountains. I love that vision and it is certainly a true idea of a sanctuary. After all, it is a lot easier to feel aligned and in tune with ourselves when we have created environments that support, nourish and replenish us. Our home, office and car environments are places that we spend a tremendous amount of time in and they influence us in all of the layers of our being.

Your environment influences you physically, emotionally, mentally and energetically, as we discussed in the section about energetic clearing (see see pages 151–162). But sanctuary also applies to our daily practices of self-care. Even if we can't buy the perfect house complete with ocean views and rose gardens we can create sanctuary in our lives in a variety of easy and cost-free ways.

One of the best ways is to create an organized space that incorporates all of the elements: earth, water, air and fire. So in your space you may want to have plants or crystals for earth; a small fountain or a fish tank for water; incense or essential oils for air; and candles for the fire element, to create the feeling of balance. When we incorporate the elements into a clean and uncluttered space, we immediately open up a space for our inspiration to soar. In such surroundings, our intuition is much easier to perceive and our joy factor is greatly enhanced.

But then there is even more. When we create sanctuaries for ourselves we energetically set the stage for our Infinite Selves to amplify their communication and provide us with big Aha! Moments, inspiration and next steps we have not thought of before. We also support our bodies by honoring them with a safe and nourishing space that can recharge our batteries.

Creating your own sanctuary is a big act of self-love and provides you with a wonderful space to call your own.

7 Love and Relationships

The seventh pillar is love and relationships. This is really referring to personal relationships in three categories: first, the love of your self; second, the love of the "God of your understanding" or higher consciousness; and third, the love of a significant other. Family relationships and friendships also come under this pillar.

You may be wondering why this pillar is last on the list. Most would think that self-love and relationships are the starting point rather than the end point. First of all, while this is written as a list in linear fashion, the principles outlined here are better represented as a circle rather than a line. Each pillar is interrelated to the others and can function individually and as a part of the whole. We will bounce through each of them throughout the day even if we are focused on becoming stronger in one in particular.

I mention the relationship pillar last because all of the others form the foundation for being able to establish and develop meaningful relationships in all categories.

By being fluent in and engaging your Aha! Factor, being aware of and managing your energy on a regular basis, having your library of support resources, making meaningful contributions, having a community of like-minded individuals that you can relate to and a personal sanctuary where you can recharge your energies, you have created a very empowering life, which will provide you with all of the nourishment and support that you need from the places where it should come from.

Establishing the first six pillars is the epitome of having self-love and respect. And they fill your tank up to the point of overflowing, enabling you to have energy to share with others without feeling dependent or depleted on your own.

How many people do you know who have few or none of the above and then attach themselves to another person in a relationship, whether it is a child, a friend, a celebrity, a coach or some other person, to fill in their blanks. When we do not have our personal pillars in place we turn to people, things, addictions and other sources to support us, and in doing so, overload our systems with confusion. No one relationship can satisfy all of our needs.

Once we have an awareness of the seven pillars and have them even marginally in place, our chances for being truly available for a fulfilling relationship sky-rocket. Why? Because when we are filled up appropriately, feel supported and have that level of access to our intuition which always guides us to the truth, we are energetically, mentally and emotionally self-sufficient. And this is the world's greatest aphrodisiac!

What would it be like if you could be in a relationship based on choice and not need? If you were really filled up, confident and self-sufficient with a surplus of energy to share with someone else because you are so well supported on your own, what could you then experience and create in a relationship? How amazing would that be?

I have seen so many clients and friends – women in particular – who turn to relationships to fill every single box and the object of their affection runs in the other direction every time. They catch the wave of the connection and then latch on, trying to control every aspect of the relationship with a variety of machinations. And once the relationship goes south, instead of taking the time to develop the other areas, they try to turn to dating sites and find another person to tick all of their boxes. In most cases this leads to the same type of relationship all over again.

Now let's talk about Divine love, which is the love and communion with the God of your understanding – whether that is an energy or a guy in the sky with a white beard – finding that relationship and fostering it is a key component to discovering your true balance. I personally see this God energy as greater than my Infinite Self, but recognize that my Infinite Self consists of the God energy. This discussion could fill a whole other book, so we won't go into great detail here. But the most important thing to do is to decide what you believe and how you want to acknowledge and communicate with that energy. Your intuition is the language of the Divine. I call it the language of answered prayer.

We all learn to ask for what we want, but we are not normally taught how to interpret answered prayer. Whether it is through engaging your intuitive, telepathic and channeling abilities, formal prayer, going out in nature, attending a church, a synagogue, a mosque or another religious institution, through art or creative endeavors, or journaling or meditation, creating an ongoing conversation with the God of your understanding is extraordinarily powerful in easing tension and helping you to move forward with ease in your life.

This relationship enables you to allow miracles to happen and discover greater capacities than you could ever access on your own with just your logical mind. It also provides a place to stabilize and find peace in a very chaotic world.

By recognizing and incorporating the seven pillars, you will be well on your way to easily creating an enlightened life that grows as you do. And this is the foundation that makes any dream a true possibility.

Chapter Eighteen

LIFE AT
FULL OPERATING POWER

A t the beginning of our time together I made a bold claim. You Matter. And Your Dreams Count. And I also stated that the world really does need what you have to offer. It was not my intention to just give you fluff or rah-rah, but instead I wanted to share with you the hidden Energetic Communication System that is here to serve you, by providing you with all of the missing pieces that are not usually shared.

It is my knowing that we have entered into a different time. We have access to more energy and interconnected resources than ever before in history. Does this really make a difference? You bet it does. From the mid-1980s I watched myself and other undiscovered sensitives work very hard to create services, products and tools to help people become more conscious, manage their energy, trust their intuition, realize their dreams and all sorts of other things. We would work tirelessly and then find a way to present our work, only to be dismissed or ridiculed or seen as crazy. So our work would go on the shelf, with our hearts broken and our confidence bruised.

Yet we kept on feeling a pull to keep going, to try again, to create something else. And most of us would do so, only to be frustrated again when the majority of the masses said no.

What was really happening was that the energetic grid and the overall group consciousness was not ready for what we were creating. But we were an integral part of the future evolution that we are now seeing today. It was as if we were Santa's elves in between high season being asked to build toys and store them for when the demand would rise during the holiday season. Just like manufacturers can't wait until November to start building Christmas inventory, the Universe asked sensitives to build the inventory, gather experiences and garner wisdom so that when the masses were ready there would be a supply for them.

The popular saying states "hindsight is 20/20" and now that we have gone through the shift of the new energy coming in and the surge of demand for all of our information and more, the technology to support our work and let people know about it is there. Publishing is much easier today and the audiences are bigger than ever.

But all of those decades of rejection, dismissiveness, lack of readiness and harsh criticism have left many of us feeling as if what we have to offer doesn't matter:

that the dreams and aspirations that we had did not count. This could not be further than the truth. It was not that you did not matter – it was that the world had some catching up to do. And now it is more than ready for you.

With the help of your Aha! Factor and the vast resources of your Energetic Communication System, you can and will be guided to the precise list of customized contributions that you can provide, which will not only make your heart sing, but provide for others as well. And money flows very easily from that irresistible combination of inspiration and contribution.

Whatever your aspirations are, there is a place for them out there. And if there were not a place, you would not be getting the inspiration to begin with. Why not take the time to truly explore what it will take to get that work of yours out to the world? Invest the time to develop the energetic systems we have discussed and begin to incorporate them into your physical world. Your dreams of contributing to others are only as good as your willingness to love and support yourself.

And the tools that we have outlined here are easy to implement and use to create powerful results way beyond what you can dream of as you now consciously tap into the power of deliberately setting intentions on the energetic grid of creation.

There is a saying that goes "If you take one step toward your dreams, your dreams will take 1,000 steps back toward you." You are needed here. God, the infinite energy, needs all of us to say "Yes!" to our dreams, because the happier we are the more we contribute to the greater consciousness with positive energy. Even if that contribution is just a smile at the tired cashier at the grocery store, it counts.

Would you be willing to step forward now? Would you be willing to dust off the ideas you have, to go and finish something you may have started and become frustrated with, or to put some focus into creating your personal foundation with your Aha! Factor and the seven pillars?

What if cracking the code is a lot easier than we think? What if all we have been missing is an awareness of an entire set of energetic tools that we are born with, yet have never been properly taught about in their entirety? That is really what has happened.

What if Life is a Lot Simpler Than We Think?

Clearly we have all been through difficult times in our lives, when we have struggled to make sense of the unexpected twists and turns. I have certainly had my share of disappointments, losses, betrayals and sad times. No one escapes these challenges entirely.

What I have found to be true for both myself and the clients I have worked with over the years is that within our biggest disappointments and challenges we have the capacity to find our greatest strengths and talents, which can be a huge contribution to ourselves and the world at large, if we are willing to share what we have garnered from them.

There is a difference between the words "simple" and "easy." When I use the word simple, I am not speaking about necessarily creating a life without challenges. However, when we are tapped into our Aha! Factor and fluent in our Energetic Communication System, having access to the wisdom and insight of our Infinite Self creates a much less complicated existence. Can you imagine experiencing spur-of-the-moment surprises and being able to just tap into that greater wisdom and trust the guidance you receive without a doubt? As we move forward that is exactly what is possible and even more.

An Exciting Time of Energetic Evolution

Many of my clients and show listeners have said to me, "Why have I not discovered this before?" or "How come we are just recognizing all of this now?"

This information is timeless and has been around for centuries. However, just as our physical world evolves and changes with all of its shifting geography and weather patterns, so our energetic world has also evolved and continues to provide us with a greater capacity to engage in it and thrive.

We have much greater access to our own energetic abilities now and the information on how to maximize them to improve our own lives, as well as the overall wellbeing of the planet, is presenting itself more than ever before in history.

These are truly exciting times because, as we comprehend and master our worlds by integrating our physical and energetic abilities with greater awareness, we have access to an infinite number of possibilities to improve our life and living.

Seeking a Fluid State of Balance

While it may be tempting to strive for a "perfect" life, I would like you to consider what your definition of "perfect" is before you do. Many perceive a "perfect" life to be one with absolutely no stress, challenges, difficult relationships, money issues and so on. However, this may not be such a good idea. Instead of trying to control circumstances, situations and the behavior of other people, when we live our lives from the inside out and engage our Aha! Factor we achieve something even better – and that is flexibility.

With all of these tools and practices what we are aiming to achieve is more of what I call a "fluid state of balance." Rather than expecting for things to be the same all of the time or requiring the same routines, people and situations to be predictable, we can choose to get in tune with our energy and higher consciousness with the highest level of "intuitive fluency" possible. This way, we can easily interpret what is ours, what is not and what we require on a minute-by-minute basis, adjusting ourselves as we go.

I remember listening to Joel Osteen talk about the ability to be flexible during a stormy time in our lives. He used the analogy of the resilience of an oak tree versus a palm tree in a hurricane. He stated that the palm tree is built for the storm as its trunk is designed to sway and bend during the intense winds of hurricanes, whereas an oak tree often topples due to its inflexible trunk. There is great power in strengthening our capacity to be resilient.

This fluid state of balance engages a high level of "conscious spontaneity" in which we are energetically nimble and willing to turn quickly and sharply, as we feel guided to do so. This is where we can begin to shine, accessing the very highest and greatest versions of what we most desire, with the most ease.

When we have a hard-and-fast plan created from only our logical minds and don't pay attention to our greater consciousness, we hit hard walls of resistance and frustration. This leads to discouragement, depression and giving up on our desires. When we are out of balance, our bodies are usually the first to let us know. We feel anxious, tired, sore, achy, sick, gain or lose weight, and may develop a myriad of other maladies to let us know that we are off track. It is all too easy to smother these symptoms with all kinds of medications and other interventions that may work temporarily, or not at all.

When we have consciously engaged our Aha! Factor and make a point to check in with it, we give ourselves access to the intelligence of our Infinite Self and can catch things that may be going out of balance in our bodies much earlier or get the best solutions for issues that already exist.

Life at Full Operating Power

When we consciously connect to our Infinite Selves and allow ourselves to operate from the inside out, we step into a capacity to create what we most desire as if from thin air. We have a better chance than ever to be able to accomplish what we hope for and even more.

I like to think of it as having access to a sort of cosmic "cloud" technology. Big companies such as Apple, Barnes & Noble and Amazon have taught the population that we really need thousands of movies, files, photos, music tracks, and apps at our fingertips. The more we need, the more space we also require. Each year the storage capacities of our phones, readers, tablets and computers grow larger and larger. At the same time, we as a society continue to demand that the devices we buy get smaller and smaller to accommodate our increasingly portable lives.

The cloud technology provides a central location for all of our files and media – in addition it gives us the ability to access every other type of media available – and this enables our computers and other devices to be much lighter and stream a lot more than they can store on their hard drives.

This is how the infinite field of consciousness works. We have access to it all, yet needn't be weighed down by it. Instead, we can navigate between our physical worlds and the energetic worlds of our Infinite Self with a seamless flow. And when this happens, anything is possible.

More and more people are coming out of their own darkness and into the light of their consciousness. And when we are filled up with this knowing and accessibility we do not have to live by so many hard-and-fast rules for how things "must" be. Instead we can have the courage to allow things to come to us, knowing that we are working in partnership with our Infinite Selves.

Let's take a look at some of the amazing benefits we gain by living our lives from the inside out. As we gain more access to our complete consciousness – the union of our Infinite and embodied selves – we have much greater capacity to lead others to their own self-discovery. We often become "way-showers" by setting an example of how we live our lives.

When we are living at full operating power from the inside out, we become a magnet for other people's curiosity. They notice our ability to flow through things without the normal levels of resistance and attachments. Self-judgment is reduced and the willingness to forgive ourselves is much greater. In fact, as we get further and further along, we start to experience life with a lot less judgment of others and ourselves.

Contribution to Others is Easier Now

In addition to being natural way-showers, we start to desire to be greater contributors to ourselves and to others. We start to ask more questions about how we can contribute. Many ask, "What is my life purpose?" It's important to note that the intentions behind those words can be quite different depending on each person's unique circumstances. For someone living from the outside in, they're looking for what will be in it for them: fame, fortune or validation that they are worthy.

But when we begin living our lives from the inside out, we have less need to define a specific purpose, a fancy title or parameters to measure ourselves up to. Instead we step into a willingness to create as we go. We choose to follow the energy and do what feels joyful at that time. This does not mean that we don't have a plan of action, but when we are intentionally uniting our energetic and physical selves we can stay in communion with our infinite consciousness and are very efficiently guided to be in the right place at the right time, with the right people. It's amazing how much more efficiently we live when we allow ourselves to be led by signs, symbols and synchronicity.

You'll notice life always leaves you breadcrumbs, if you pay attention.

As we master these ways, we enter into a new time of allowance where we are willing to let our good appear in our lives. We no longer need to control everything when we are aware of the unlimited access our consciousness provides us.

Our Biggest Critics Can Be Our Greatest Messengers

Inevitably, when we decide to think and choose differently than what many consider to be "normal," we will encounter those who criticize our choices. But instead of losing our temper or getting discouraged we can choose to see the skeptics in our lives as messengers. They show us the way to reach deeper into our consciousness and shore up our resolve to live our lives from the guidance within. Skeptics help us to remember to check in and see what is true for ourselves.

Not everyone needs to be like us in order to validate that we are on the right track. As we become stronger and more confident in our connection to our Infinite

Selves we can get to the place where we are able to allow everyone to be who they desire to be and that does not have to influence who we are or the choices that we make. We are no longer thrown off for long by other people's actions and we can then honor and allow others to engage their own free will, points of view and choices without judgment or a mission to change them.

Integration of Our Energetic and Physical Worlds

We are now ready to fully embrace our physical world with energetic awareness that delivers a powerful experience to us. We can truly live from the inside out. Our tangible day-to-day experiences are wonderfully enhanced by our increasing awareness of our Infinite Self and our conscious communication with it. We no longer have to feel alone or as confused by what is going on in our lives.

It also becomes much easier to trust that even though we may not be able to see the entire map, we have a powerful force guiding us and providing us with the most efficient route that will reap the richest rewards. This trust and willingness to let go and work in concert with our Infinite Selves opens up our capacity to attract and achieve more than we can ever imagine. And at the very least we will have an easier time of it with a lot less angst and anxiety.

The World Changes as We Do

The more we allow ourselves to become energetically integrated and energetically healthy, the more influence we have on the outside world. When this happens, our creativity flourishes and our cup overflows, fortifying us with a much greater capacity to contribute to others.

We see amazing shifts happen in our world as we ignite these changes within ourselves. We access the new grid of energy and unleash insight and influence to which we have never had access before.

We have a much higher level of compassion for others and can release the need to control, without feeling like we must force our own way on others.

We are living from the inside out and this is what illumination truly is all about. The final point I will make here is that there is no "perfect way"; these are all simply guidelines. We each have the freedom to create as we go, and freedom is the ultimate gift to ourselves – because when we are free to be who we are, we can then accept others' freedom as well. And the world can flow magically from there.

Energetic fluency applied to our physical world provides us with our greatest opportunity for genuine joy in our lives. It is my hope that you will gather what feels right for you from our time together here and put it to work in your own world. You truly can have exactly what you desire. You do not have to suffer and ratchet yourself down to play it safe. There is so much more that is here for you and with these tools you have the keys to access it all. Be patient, be consistent and honor your curiosity, it will always lead you to even greater possibilities.

Here's to You,
   To Your Light,
   To Your Freedom
You truly can have exactly what you want. You absolutely deserve it to. And when you engage your Aha! Factor, anything is possible!

Thank you for reading!

Dear Reader,

I hope that you enjoyed The Aha! Factor. *All the information in this book I have collected personally along my own path and refined through trial and error as well as by working with thousands of clients around the world.*

One thing I know for sure: it is much more fun to explore these principles with people of like mind, and I would like to invite you to join our Aha! Moments Global Community at www.TheAhaWay.com. *Here you will find my blog, tips and tools, as well as access to online courses and info on* The Aha! Moments Radio Show *and on how to join our bustling communities on social media. We would love to have you and if you join us we will make you feel right at home!*

Through the years I have received so many emails on the topics in the book and so many listeners have called into our radio shows letting me know what makes their heart sing, what they would like to learn more about and what they would like to see improve. As an author I would love to hear from you. You can write me at Mari@TheAhaWay.com

Finally, I'd like to ask you a favor. If you are so inclined I would very much appreciate it if you could take the time to review The Aha! Factor *online. Your feedback is so valuable as I develop new programs, shows and future books. And your insight provides valuable information for other readers.*

Thank you so much for spending time with me.

In gratitude,

Mariana

WATKINS
Sharing Wisdom Since
1893

The story of Watkins Publishing dates back to March 1893, when John M. Watkins, a scholar of esotericism, overheard his friend and teacher Madame Blavatsky lamenting the fact that there was nowhere in London to buy books on mysticism, occultism or metaphysics. At that moment Watkins was born, soon to become the home of many of the leading lights of spiritual literature, including Carl Jung, Rudolf Steiner, Alice Bailey and Chögyam Trungpa.

Today our passion for vigorous questioning is still resolute. With over 350 titles on our list, Watkins Publishing reflects the development of spiritual thinking and new science over the past 120 years. We remain at the cutting edge, committed to publishing books that change lives.

DISCOVER MORE ...

Read our blog

Watch and listen to
our authors in action

Sign up to
our mailing list

JOIN IN THE CONVERSATION

Our books celebrate conscious, passionate, wise and happy living.
Be part of the community by visiting

www.watkinspublishing.com